Current Trends and Traditions in Management Accounting Case Analysis

Fifth Edition

Gary Spraakman

CAPTUS PRESS

Current Trends and Traditions in
Management Accounting Case Analysis, Fifth edition

© 2007 by Gary Spraakman and Captus Press Inc.

First edition, Summer 1994
Fifth edition, Spring 2007

Captus Press Inc.
Mail: Units 14 & 15
1600 Steeles Avenue West
Concord, Ontario
Canada   L4K 4M2
Telephone: (416) 736–5537
Fax: (416) 736–5793
E-mail: info@captus.com
Internet: www.captus.com

Library and Archives Canada Cataloguing in Publication

Spraakman, Gary
    Current trends and traditions in management accounting case analysis / Gary Spraakman. — 5th ed.

ISBN 978-1-55322-130-2

    1. Managerial accounting — Case studies.   I. Title

HF5657.4.S67 2007   658.15'11   C2007-902248-0

Canada [*|*] *We acknowledge the financial support of the Government of Canada through the Book Publishing Industry Development Program (BPIDP) for our publishing activities.*

0 9 8 7 6 5 4 3 2 1
Printed in Canada

Contents

Acknowledgments

I have many people to thank. My students deserve special thanks for allowing me to test these cases. I often learned more about the cases from their responses.

Specifically, I thank the following: Leslie Sanders for her editorial assistance; Elden Gardner, editor of the *Journal of Accounting Case Research*, for his encouragement and support with case research; Elizabeth Gayford for her response to the case, PC Board; and Simia Pir for her assistance with the Yoour University and Electronic Process Equipment cases.

This book of cases is directed at students who are taking a course in management accounting. The materials presuppose introductory courses in management accounting and financial accounting.

The book, intended to supplement management accounting textbooks, has six purposes. The first two are typical and related: (1) to supply cases that demand the application of management accounting techniques, and (2) to introduce students to more practical situations than those typical of most textbooks. The next two purposes differentiate this casebook from others: (3) to provide material that keeps abreast of changes to practice, and (4) to familiarize students with the traditions of case analysis in management accounting.

The cases included in this book respond to the difficulties our students' experience when case analysis is demanded of them. I believe their difficulties occur for a number of reasons:

- Students spend up to 50 percent of their time reading and digesting the material before they do any thinking and writing. It is as if case authors advocate using long cases as teaching devices in order to allow adequate data for decision making, but the effort required to digest the case may leave the student little time for in-depth analysis.

- The case approach is learned, but not taught. Many students are forced to learn the case approach in a very general and imprecise fashion, almost like osmosis.

- Although students can identify issues or problems, they have difficulty with analysis; i.e., they have trouble discerning related themes, causes, and effects, among issues, which is the objective of case analysis.

- Recommendations are readily suggested, but they are neither explained nor justified. When cases require implementation planning, recommendations are outlined in the most rudimentary fashion.

- Case responses tend to display a superficial understanding of case questions. This is probably a result of the other weaknesses and not a separate weakness.

I believe these weaknesses have two roots. First, the teaching of the case approach is implicit, and case analysis skills appear elusive to students. Second, long, verbose cases encourage superficial thinking because there is insufficient time for in-depth considerations.

These weaknesses, and my desire to remove them, suggest the final two purposes of this book: (5) to provide short cases so as to minimize reading time and to encourage greater depth of analysis, and (6) to teach case analysis explicitly and provide feedback for learning.

This is an exciting time in which to design a management accounting casebook. Management accounting is in a period of transition. Since 1987 when Johnson and Kaplan (1987) called attention to the stagnation of management accounting practices, there have been many changes such as activity-based costing and target costing. During the past decade an increasing number of companies have been impacted by information technology in terms of computerized transaction processing and electronic telecommunications such as that done with the Internet, intranet, and extranet. For competitive reasons, companies have had to change from manual and then mainframe systems to what have been called enterprise resource planning (ERP) systems. An ERP system has a common database or data warehouse that links together all systems in all parts of a company, including, for example, capital budgeting with financial, control, manufacturing, sales, fixed assets, inventory, human resources modules, etc. An ERP system, by linking all systems through a data warehouse, allows a company to manage its operations holistically.

A second impact of ERP systems has been a general shift to manage at the activity level rather than at the more abstract level of financial transactions. This means that management accounting, with its focus on activities, can be most effective when it is used with ERP systems to incorporate the activity level for costing and performance measurement. To be effective an ERP system will contain an extensive chart of accounts or codes for activities such as accurate recording and tracking of activities, revenues and costs. The coding incorporates stable entities of a business, such as divisions, plants, stores, and warehouses. At a detailed level there are codes for functions such as finance, production, sales, marketing, and materials management. There are also the traditional financial account codes, such as assets, liabilities, revenues, and expenses, and the central ERP feature of coding processes, activities, and subactivities. There must be consistent coding among all parts of a company in order for them to relate to one another.

As the ERP system incorporates activities in terms of quantities of resources, including labour, a record of resource use is maintained. Therefore, performance can be measured in physical terms and compared to standards, which allows for the calculation of variances. This performance measurement at the activity level serves as a feedback system on efficiency and effectiveness. The confusion caused by abstract monetary measures is erased, and what is actually happening with the conversion of resources into goods and services can be seen. ERP systems have the potential to change management accounting systems with more detailed, more integrated, and faster produced information.

The information technology context of contemporary organizations has been incorporated into many of the cases contained in this book, which has two parts.

Section I describes management accounting case analysis. The second chapter explains the type of judgment that management accounting case analysis requires. Chapter 3 contains a sample case that demonstrates the application of the case approach, and chapter 4 explains two approaches to case marking. A guided practice of case analysis is given in chapter 5. Chapter 6 introduces an approach to activity costing.

In Section II there are 35 cases for practice. Their contexts come from various industries, manufacturing, service, non-profit, and government. Taken together, they demand most of the management accounting techniques discussed at the introductory or intermediate levels of management accounting.

This fifth edition introduces 13 new cases that test students on contemporary management accounting techniques (balanced scorecard, cost of quality report, performance measurement, value chain) within emerging organizational contexts (best-in-class, business models, customer relationship management, enterprise resource planning systems, outsourcing, strategy, and total value creation).

REFERENCE

Kaplan, R.E., and H.T. Johnson, *Relevance Lost: The Rise and Fall of Management Accounting* (Boston, MA: Harvard Business School Press, 1987).

SECTION I

The Case Approach

## CHAPTER 1

Developing Judgment

Case analysis is both teachable and learnable. It involves the use of judgment in complex practical situations, both in regard to the identification and analyses of issues, the choice of appropriate techniques, and recommendations for resolving the issues. Issues, analyses, and recommendations are the focus of this chapter. Techniques will have been learned in management accounting courses.

EDUCATIONAL OBJECTIVES, AND WAYS OF THINKING

Understanding the educational objectives of the case approach will help students pursue these assignments effectively. The case objectives come from Bloom's taxonomy (Bloom et al., 1956), a taxonomy that accounting educators have accepted (Clevenger, 1990).

Following are Bloom's educational objectives:

1. **Knowledge**. Recalling previously learned material. Students need to remember facts, principles, and steps in a sequence. A sample question that seeks out student knowledge would be, "Define variable and fixed costs."

2. **Comprehension**. The understanding of material presented in a course. At this level students explain, interpret, translate to a new form or symbol system, and extrapolate. A sample question would be, "Explain an operating statement along the lines of variable costing."

3. **Application**. The ability to use learning in other situations. Students are to use abstractions such as concepts, principles, rules, theories, and laws to find solutions to new problems. A sample question would be, "Use the contribution margin approach to explain the level of sales needed to break even." Numerical exercises and problems at the back

of management accounting textbook chapters tend to be applications.

4. **Analysis**. The capability for breaking content into component parts in order to understand the relationships among parts. A sample question would be, "Compare and contrast the operating statement for the company under absorption costing with direct costing."

5. **Synthesis**. Putting together of parts to form a new whole. Students use what they have learned to produce new products such as themes, speeches, or research proposals. A sample question would be, "From the evidence in the case, discuss how, with an expansionary, high-end-of-the-market strategy, the company became bankrupt."

6. **Evaluation**. The ability to judge the value of material in light of a specific purpose using given criteria. Students make quantitative and qualitative judgments about the extent to which material and methods satisfy criteria. A sample question would be, "Using the criteria of relevant and timely information for making decisions, evaluate the division's new information system compared to that which existed previously."

The case approach for management accounting presupposes that students possess a high degree of knowledge, comprehension and application skills, the first three of the six ascending educational objectives in the taxonomy. The primary focus of the case approach for this book is on analysis and synthesis.

An example of a response that reveals analysis skills might be one in which the student considers the operating statements of an organization in comparison to the industry and realizes "the organization is performing more poorly than the industry average."

More specifically, the student would exhibit analytical skill if he or she determined the following:

- the contribution of all 12 sales regions;
- eight of the 12 sale regions were profitable, and four were not;
- the unprofitable sales regions were in remote parts of the country, with higher turnover, especially among managers who did not consider themselves truly part of the firm; and
- few managers of the unprofitable regions had promotions to corporate office jobs.

Synthesis builds upon analysis and it asks, "What does it all mean?" Continuing with our example, a student could synthesize the evidence to explain that the poor profitability in the remote sales areas is a result of poor motivation, caused by the organization's neglect of the remote sales areas. As a consequence of this neglect, there is a higher than average turnover, and the managers do not believe themselves to be integral parts of the company. Synthesis is the skill by which evidence is linked together, creating a plausible explanation.

DEFINITION OF A CASE QUESTION

Students need to begin with a clear understanding of the case method. Thompson and Strickland (1980) provide an insightful definition and explanation of a case:

> A case sets forth, in a factual manner, the conditions and circumstances surrounding a particular managerial situation or series of events in an organization. It may include descriptions of the industry and its competitive conditions, the organization's background, its products and markets, the attitudes and personalities of the key people involved, production facilities, the work climate, the organization structure, marketing methods, and the external environment, together with whatever pertinent financial, production, accounting, sales, and market information upon which management has to depend. It may concern any kind of organization — profit-seeking business, or a public service institution.

The written description of the practical situation is called the case question. A good case question offers as real a practice situation as can be achieved short of the "real thing." It puts students at the scene of the action and familiarizes them with the actors and the contexts for their actions.

There are four objectives with the case method; awareness of these objectives will help students understand the process of case analysis. The first objective is to help the student learn to put management accounting techniques into practice. The second is to turn the student into an active learner rather than simply a passive accumulator of information. Case analysis helps students to acquire the habit of diagnosing issues, analyzing and evaluating alternatives, and formulating workable plans of action. The third objective is to train students to work out answers for themselves, rather than relying upon the authority of the professor or a textbook. Finally, case analysis provides students with exposure to a range of organizations and management accounting situations, which otherwise would take a lifetime to experience personally. The exposure to a variety of situations will help students make career choices, as well as assist them in their careers.

RESPONDING TO A CASE QUESTION

This section will discuss the component parts of the case method and the student's responsibilities in completing an analysis. The focus of the section will be on helping the student to respond appropriately to a case question. As well, this section will provide some practical "how to" advice. Based on the suggestions in this section, and with practice, students should be able to develop an approach to case analysis that they are comfortable applying to various case questions.

There are two components to case analysis: the case question and the case response.

Case Question

The case question establishes the scenario or "story" of an organization. Typically, it includes characters — managers, workers, customers, etc., and a setting that will be some part or perspective of an organization. Cases can depict any type of organization, and there are many possible scenarios, given the number of management accounting topics and the equally large number of organizational types.

No matter what the scenario, there are issues or problems that must be resolved. An issue exists when there is a gap between expectations and actual performance in an area of an organization. For example, management accounting teaches students that organizations should have budgets for operational guidance. When a scenario states that an organization does not have a budget, then this is an issue.

The scenario of a case question will generally contain many issues revealed in comments made by case characters, findings by case characters, trends or ratios contained in financial statements, financial summaries, and industry comparisons. Identification of issues at first may be difficult. Through practice, however, students will become proficient at identifying as well as linking them.

One way to identify issues is to determine those attributes of the hypothetical organization that differ from the accounting and management practices that are taught as correct. Another method is to identify those attributes that lead to less than optimal economic performance. Examples include declining sales in comparison to those of competitors, missed profit opportunities, managers insufficiently profit-oriented, inaccurate budgeting, misleading cost accounting, ineffective sales incentives, and a failure to develop replacements for maturing products.

Imagine a case where two managers did not get along personally: a lumber manufacturing organization's log purchasing manager and mill manager refused to co-operate with each other. Their inability to co-operate led to a shortage of appropriate logs for a certain large and important order, and caused other production scheduling problems as well. There are three issues in this example. First, personal conflict was affecting operations. Second, scheduling difficulties occurred. Third, management was unable to develop the necessary systems for scheduling that would work despite personal conflicts. For this example, the *root* issue was that "management was not able to develop the necessary systems." The other two issues, "personal conflict" and "scheduling deficiencies," are due to the lack of appropriate systems. With proper systems for scheduling that would work despite personal conflicts, "personal conflict" and "scheduling deficiencies" would not be problematic.

In addition to the scenario, the case question may contain a "required" that asks the student to do something. Typically, the "required" is the link between the case question and the case response. A required can be directed or non-directed, depending on the amount of direction provided to the student. Students should take special care to correctly understand the "required" before formulating the case response.

Learning to read a case efficiently and effectively is the key to good case analysis. Students should develop approaches that suit their typical reading strategies. Nevertheless, a recommended

approach is to read the case quickly in order to get a sense of the context, and then to re-read it carefully and in detail. If one uses this approach, it is advisable to read the "required" before the second reading of the case. Re-reading with the "required" in mind allows one to discriminate between what is essential in the case and what is not.

Case Response

The case response is the student's answer to the case question. There is no one right or definitive answer to a case question. However, a student should not conclude that there are no wrong answers. Case responses differ because of differing identification of issues and analysis of relations among issues, differing determinations of what the root or underlying issues are, and differing development of recommendations to resolve the root issues and, in turn, the other issues. Although a variety of responses are valid at every stage, some, clearly, are incorrect.

The case response format is not fixed; typically it depends on the case question. However, using a simple, standardized form will improve case responses and provide a context for unambiguous marking. It is recommended that students use the issue–analyses–recommendations framework, deciding for themselves, according to the particular case, whether to use the three headings or to combine the first and second or the second and third. The three parts are described and analyzed below.

Issues Problems or issues are those things that are wrong with the organization.

Students should read a case question once or twice to gather its essence. While reading, it is helpful to identify the issues by circling or highlighting them or by taking notes. Then, the student reviews these identified issues, adding to them any issues revealed by related analysis of financial statements and other supplementary information supplied.

In order to "size up" the root issues, it is essential to have a clear understanding of the organization and its issues. This analysis can be accomplished in two steps.

First, make a list of the issues. Arrange and assemble similar issues into groups. Explain the relationships among the groups or categories that emerge at this stage. The groupings should be governed by two criteria. First, same or related issues should be grouped together; for example, all issues related to inaccurate financial information would go into one group. Second, associations among issues within a group should be specified;

for example, inaccurate accounting information led to poor decisions on inventory orders.

Second, the relationship among the categories must be explained. This explanation should reveal the real issues. Once they are disclosed, the real or root issues should be linked in a logical sequence. This listing should show the dependent relationship between the other issues and their root issues. Care should be taken to account for any specific requests that arise because of the role assigned to the student. The request may specify the perspective the student takes in assessing the issues. Requests may also be understood as additional issues.

The primary reason for grouping and ranking issues is to detect the underlying pattern of root issues. Sometimes, issues may also be the same as the root issues. In others, the detection may be more difficult. For example, consider a manufacturing firm with several problems: sales are not growing as expected; customers are returning products; customer satisfaction with the product quality is declining; and rework has increased. The root issue, lack of quality control, causes the other issues. Specifically, there was no quality control in the production process. The absence of quality control led to more rework and to the shipping of defective products, which the customers then returned or refused to buy again, and persuaded others not to buy.

It is identification of the root issues that enables the student to specify succinctly what is wrong with an organization. Proper identification requires close reading of the entire case, including appendices. Some information may have little or no bearing on the issues. As in the real-life situations that case analysis seeks to emulate, the student must sift carefully through all discernible aspects of a situation in order to determine which are relevant.

Analysis Analysis and issue identification are highly related. Analysis requires a thorough assessment of why an issue arose or exists, how various issues relate to each other, and which issues lead to others and are, therefore, the most crucial to an understanding of the root issues. The analysis section includes required quantitative analysis, e.g., capital budgeting and variance analysis. The analysis discloses how well essential organizational functions are working, e.g., planning, controlling, and management information systems. Analysis can also reveal, when necessary, the strengths and weaknesses of the organization. The analysis may vary in complexity. It can be as simple as listing

the supporting issues, or as complex as finding the root or underlying issues.

Some case questions have a singular answer either because of the context or because of the "required." Other case questions lend themselves to a series of alternatives for solving issues. Alternatives should be individually meaningful and mutually exclusive. For example, for a business with serious profit problems, one alternative might be to reduce costs and focus on the core business. Another alternative might be to close the business and sell the assets and inventories. Each alternative must be explained and justified as an answer, and if appropriate, its advantages and disadvantages should be discussed.

Recommendations The recommendations are a student's approach to remedying the root issues. They should be selected from the alternatives discussed in the analysis section. In the course of resolving the root issues, the recommendations must also resolve most of the other issues. Recommendations should be action oriented, decisive and unambiguous; i.e., they should explicitly resolve the issues, assign responsibilities and set deadlines.

It may be suitable to include a conclusion that deals with implementation, especially with timing, and the assignment of responsibilities that arise out of the recommendations.

For the example, with respect to the organization with profit problems, a student might recommend cost cutting and focus on the core business alternative. The student should follow the selection of this alternative by specifying how it would resolve the profit problems, and by suggesting an implementation plan. The implementation should detail which costs are to be cut, by whom, and with what consequences. It should detail which businesses are to be eliminated and which ones are to remain. If sufficient information is available, the recommendations should be quantified, showing the expected profit improvement.

In the report writing stage, it is often more time efficient and effective to identify, analyze, and make recommendations for each root issue individually. It is nevertheless essential to show the integration of the various issues within the case. Whatever the approach, it should be justified as the most appropriate for the case question.

TYPES OF CASES

Cases can be differentiated according to three characteristics: (1) the extent to which the "required" directs students, (2) the number of possible correct responses, and (3) the number of management accounting techniques evoked by the analysis. These characteristics are often interrelated.

The case's "required" can be direct or non-direct. A directed case leaves little opportunity for the student to decide the issues that need addressing, e.g., "calculate the net present value of a capital project." A non-directed case is just the opposite. Students must figure out the issues, e.g., "make recommendations to improve profitability."

The degree of directness of the "required" often relates to the number of possible correct responses. In non-directed cases, students can choose more than one way of seeing or grouping the issues, and so will arrive at a variety of appropriate sets of issues–analyses–recommendations. Consequently, there probably will be many correct responses, or solutions. At the other extreme, in a directed case, there are a restricted number of correct responses, possibly only one.

The number of management accounting techniques incorporated into a case can vary from as few as two to as many as 10 or 12. As a rule, the more techniques are used, the larger the number of possible acceptable responses is, and the less directed the case is.

This book consists largely of directed cases, each employing two or three management accounting techniques, and inviting several possible correct responses. This level of complexity is appropriate for intermediate management accounting students, and it is a step towards preparing students for minimally directed, multi-technique cases with many possible correct responses.

WRITING THE CASE RESPONSE

The role that the student is to play usually is established in the case question, sometimes in the "required." Also specified will be for whom the student is working. For example, the student may be a controller working closely with the president to determine funding for a capital project. As controller, the student must write a report to the president.

The case response in this context is prepared as a report. Typically it contains an introduction, and sections for issues, analysis, recommendations, and conclusion. The student should include a covering memorandum transmitting the report from the role played to the person or position for whom the work is being done. A short paragraph noting that the report is enclosed and linking it with the "required" is usually in order.

THE ROLE OF THE STUDENT

The essence of the student's role in case analysis is to diagnose and size up an organization's situation and to think through what, if anything, should be done. The student identifies and analyzes the root and other issues, and proposes recommendations to resolve them. In formulating their analyses and recommendations, students must make assumptions about how the issues relate to one another. Their assumptions must be realistic, given the context of the question.

After reading this chapter it is important for students to recognize that cases will differ. Understanding the differences will enable them to be successful with case analysis. For the level of case analysis intended with this book, there are three ways of differentiating cases.

First, cases can be differentiated as to educational objective. Students will be tested for analysis or synthesis. Analysis requires students to break content into component parts and then to understand the relationships among those parts. Alternatively, synthesis requires students to take the parts to form a new whole. A case could test students for their ability to undertake analysis or synthesis or both. Of course, for the management accounting techniques for which they are responsible, students must be competent as to the educational objectives of knowledge, comprehension, and application.

Second, cases can be differentiated by the number of issues, which could vary from a few to many. All issues must be considered, either on their own or by grouping or synthesis. Thus, cases with more issues tend to be more demanding then cases with fewer issues.

Third, cases differ by the directedness of the "required." Directed cases tend to be easier for students.

This casebook contains cases that tend to need analysis and synthesis. They contain relatively few issues, and they tend to be directed.

REFERENCES

Bloom, B.S., M.D. Englehart, G.J. Furst, W.H. Hill, and D.R. Krathwohl, *Taxonomy of Educational Objectives: The Classification of Educational Goals* (New York, NY: David McKay Co., 1956).

Clevenger, T.B., "The Cognitive Domain of Educational Objectives: A Model for Future Accounting Education," presented to the American Accounting Association, 1990 annual meeting, Toronto, ON.

Thompson, A.A. Jr., and A.J. Strickland III, *Strategic Formulation and Implementation: Tasks of the General Manager* (Dallas, TX: Business Publications, 1980).

CHAPTER 2

An Example and a Demonstration

The chapter presents a case and the steps of case analysis. The case in this chapter is qualitative; judgment is necessary to ascertain and assess the various issues. Cases can, of course, also be quantitative. Most cases in management accounting include a mix of qualitative and quantitative data. Read this case to see how a response is developed.

ONE-BIG-FIRM LTD.

The example case question shown in Exhibit 1 is typical of traditional management accounting cases. The handwritten notes in the margin and underlining are suggested techniques for identifying and analyzing issues.

EXHIBIT 1: CASE QUESTION

Established in 1981, ONE-BIG-FIRM (ONE) has three operating divisions (Coszy House, Dishland, and Hammer and Nail) and a centralized purchasing and warehousing division. This arrangement led to profitable operations during the 1980s and 1990s. ONE expanded at a more rapid rate than could the three operating divisions if they were independent.

? Unusual organizational arrangement

During the 1990s, market conditions changed; retail expansion slowed. Many imitated ONE's volume approach, and some of these competitors have been doing better jobs at controlling costs. Market shares have declined, with the level of profitability falling for all three operating divisions.

— profit problems
— loss of customers

There are feelings throughout ONE that the product markets have matured, and that the future will not be pleasant for those who remain with the firm.

— morale (assumption)
— need new products or markets

Coszy House is a national volume retailer of upholstered and wooden household furniture. It has a strong market following and an 11 percent market share. Most of the furniture is purchased in the eastern part of the country and sold under the manufacturer's name. Inventory is purchased in advance and shipped to ONE's central warehouse. Later, the furniture is shipped directly to customers. Trucks move inventory both from the manufacturer to the central warehouse and from the central warehouse to the regional warehouses. The shipments to the regional warehouses are co-ordinated with periodic and planned sales events.

Why not ship direct?
— expensive
— high cost

Dishland is the division that sells a broad range of quality dishes and glassware. The products come from Great Britain and other European countries. On a quarterly basis, buyers from the Central Purchasing and Warehouse (CPW) division visit the manufacturers. The purchases are received at a major port, immediately shipped and initially stored in the central warehouse, and then shipped to the regional warehouses. After a customer orders, the merchandise comes from a regional warehouse. Later, the customer picks up the ordered merchandise. Sales are highly seasonal with 70 percent occurring during the last three months of each year. Except for special promotions which account for 40 percent of annual sales, the demand is highly predictable. Moreover, there is little price or delivery time competition. Dishland is a large distributor in its field.

✓

EXHIBIT 1...cont'd

Hammer and Nail is a hardware chain with a product line that includes a full range of hardware supplies and equipment. With expansion, Hammer and Nail developed a high volume specialized warehouse facility in the central warehouse. Purchasing in volume and then repackaging into units sufficiently small for the stores led to substantial savings. This resulted in the division obtaining a 9 percent market share compared to 3 percent for the second largest competitor. The central warehouse stores hardware products before shipment to regional warehouses.

— strong competition

Why?
— bad
— Unusual unresponsive to customers

The regional warehouses connect the stores through the central warehouse computer with direct order communication lines and, thus, orders can be quickly processed. In recent years, many hardware dealers have formed buyer co-operatives to exert pressure on manufacturers to provide lower prices. Also, manufacturers can provide smaller quantities per order through technological innovations.

The three operating divisions detail their monthly sales budgets one year in advance; CPW uses these budgets as a basis for planning its purchasing activities. CPW makes purchases to meet budgeted sales and to ensure adequate inventory in all regional warehouses for all three operating divisions. The rigidity of CPW's inventory requirements has benefited ONE through favourable prices on purchases to the extent of 2 percent on sales. Yet the fears of excess inventories and the difficulties in adjusting after the commencement of the fiscal year have encouraged CPW to purchase only those products that, based on past performance, are sure to sell. Operating divisions perceive this rigidity as the reason for losing opportunities to meet changes in market demand.

— serious problem

There is a financial division responsible for all accounting, treasury, computer systems, and financial control activities. ONE places all other corporate functions under a vice-president of corporate services, e.g., personnel and labour relations, advertising, legal counsel, and insurance.

A basic policy of ONE is the charging out of non-operating or overhead costs. The operating divisions receive CPW costs based on sales volumes; these allocated costs have steadily increased from 6.3 percent five years ago to 12.7 percent. Comparable services cost about 3.5 percent of competitor sales. Non-operating divisions can pass on certain costs to the operating divisions with few restrictions. However, the operating divisions consider their actual performance to be before allocated costs.

— no incentive to minimize costs
— CPW is out of cost control

— bad

For the past seven years, the costs of CPW have increased at a more rapid rate than the costs and revenues of the operating divisions. The actual CPW costs have exceeded the budgeted costs in nearly each of those years. The operating divisions are unhappy with the responsiveness of CPW to their requirements. For the right product at the right price, CPW requires longer lead times than its more responsive competitors. To obtain greater responsiveness, two divisions have established expediting functions. All operating divisions have hired additional staff to help the co-ordination of activities with CPW. The co-ordinating employees duplicate some functions within the CPW division.

— CPW is out of cost control
— excess employees a symptom
— excess warehouse space

A recent study identified a need for only 75 percent of the warehouse space in the central warehouse. Of this required space, Coszy House uses two thirds, while the other two divisions use the other one third. Management has calculated similar utilization for the regional warehouses. Moreover, the president requested a national trucking firm to study ONE's transportation requirements. The trucking firm proposed for $5.2 million a year to move all merchandise from manufacturers to regional warehouses/stores. This approach would lead to substantial savings. The back hauls, i.e., the trips that the trucks make back to the central warehouse, would no longer be empty. The president believes that competitive tendering would further reduce the present quoted price.

— investigate trucking offer

— excess costs
— tenders

Required

The president has asked you to identify methods for improving profitability. Prepare a report for the president including your findings, analysis, and recommendations.

Understanding the Case Question

The student is responsible for responding to the case's "required." In order to do so, the student must understand the case and its inherent issues. In order to identify the root issues, the student must start by identifying what appear to be the issues.

It is a helpful practice to gather the issues by reviewing one's case question margin notes and underlining. Case questions are always lean on detail, and thus, the student will always need to make reasonable assumptions for missing details. The following list of issues is not exhaustive.

Profitability	Profitability has declined.
Competition	Competitors have replicated the successful market approach of the 1970s and 1980s, and often more cost effectively.
Responsiveness	The retail stores are not responsive to customers.
Budgeting	Budgeting is done far in advance, with little ability to adjust for changing market conditions.
Inefficiency	ONE is paying for trucks running empty on the back haul. Financial leadership is missing. Cost control is poor.
Warehousing and purchasing costs	These have grown faster than sales and other costs, and faster than competitors' expenses for the same outlays.
Staffing	To offset the poor service of CPW, the operating divisions hire extra employees.
Excess warehouse space	Current operating methods do not require 25 percent of the space.
Overhead	Operating divisions receive overhead costs on an actual cost basis, which provides no incentive for the overhead units to minimize costs.
Profit measurement	There is a lack of agreement on the measurement of operating profits.

Warehousing	Two levels of warehouses increase costs, with no additional improvement in service.
Trucking	Investigate the trucking offer, as it is a means of reducing costs. Seek tenders.

ONE has some problems, which if left untended will lead to destruction. The overriding issue is that the current marketing strategy — central purchasing and warehousing — is no longer valid. Although the major issue is not directly stated, it is the theme that links many issues listed above. For example, the cost advantages of central purchasing and warehousing no longer offset the disadvantages of rigidity and unresponsiveness to demand, as the low profitability attests.

Other issues include the following:

- CPW is too expensive.
- There is unutilized warehouse space.
- There is surplus staff.
- There is no strategic plan.
- There is little concern for profitability.
- Financial leadership is missing.
- Morale is bad.

After arriving at an understanding of the major issue, and sketching out the analysis section, the next step is to write the case response. A case response example is given in Exhibit 2. It is just a possible response of many to the ONE case question's "required."

CONCLUDING COMMENTS

The case method replicates real-life situations in a simplified way. It allows students to display their ability to apply what they have learned in management accounting courses. This chapter showed students how to write a case response without time constraints. In an examination setting, with time constraints, students may have difficulty identifying as many issues, and their analyses and recommendations may be more superficial.

EXHIBIT 2: CASE RESPONSE

(Memorandum)

TO: Ms. A.A. Smith, President

FROM: John Raj, Accountant

SUBJECT: Profitability Opportunities

Please find attached my report specifying the profit improvement opportunities you have requested. The report includes a discussion of the problems solved by the recommendations.

Sincerely,
John Raj

(Report)

Introduction

ONE-BIG-FIRM Ltd. (ONE), a diversified retail firm with activities across Canada, has three operating divisions and centralized purchasing and warehousing. Senior managers are concerned with the level of profitability. The president requested the report for identifying profit opportunities.

Issue Identification

As requested, I reviewed ONE's operations. I analyzed many issues for common threads and causal relationships. Seven major or root issues emerged:

- The current marketing strategy — central purchasing and warehousing — is no longer valid.
- CPW is too expensive.
- There is unutilized warehouse space.
- There are surplus employees.
- There is no strategic plan.
- There is little concern for profitability.
- Morale is bad.

Analysis and Recommendations

1. **The marketing strategy is inappropriate**.
   The marketing strategy is obsolete. Although the central purchasing and warehousing approach worked well in the past, competitors have imitated ONE, and controlled costs. Rather than being an advantage, central purchasing and warehousing is now more expensive than alternative approaches employed by competitors. Moreover, the current marketing approach is rigid and non-responsive to the needs of customers.

   Recommendations: Develop a strategy for getting ONE out of the current strategic problem. This will involve primarily a marketing strategy that stresses customer responsiveness and market share.

2. **CPW is too expensive.**
   Central purchasing and warehousing cost 12.7 percent of sales compared to 3.5 percent for equivalent services with competitors. There is a 2 percent advantage on purchases with central purchasing. The total disadvantage is 7.2 percent of sales.

   Recommendations: Decentralize the purchasing and warehousing operations. This will mean dismantling CPW, and restructuring those functions to something comparable to the competitors of the operating divisions. The result, reduced costs to competitor levels, will add to profits.

3. **There is underused warehouse space**.
   Lease the 25 percent vacant space. Warehouse requirements could further decline if vendors ship directly to regional warehouses or retail stores.

   Recommendations: Sub-lease excess warehouse space. With the decentralization of purchasing and warehousing, there will be even less need for the warehouses. The most profitable option may be to sell the central warehouse and require vendors to ship to regional warehouses or to retail stores.

4. **There are surplus employees**.
   Because of the poor service by the central purchasing and warehousing division, the operating divisions have hired expediting staff. If CPW was responsive to the operating divisions, the expediters would not be needed.

   Recommendations: Re-deploy expediting employees and reduce costs.

5. **There is no strategic plan**.
   ONE has been blindly pursuing one strategy without the preparation for eventual modification or replacement of that strategy — central purchasing and warehousing — when it lost its viability.

   Recommendations: Develop a strategic plan to prepare for the future.

6. **There is little concern for profitability**.
   ONE has seen its level of profitability decline significantly in recent years, but it has not proposed serious remedies. In addition, cost control has never been seriously considered, as shown by the allocation of actual overhead costs to the operating divisions.

   Recommendations: Profitability should be given more importance. Develop a financial orientation. Establish financial goals with budgets and plans. Use incentives to obtain higher profitability.

7. **Morale is bad**.
   The decline in profitability and the relative improvement of competitors have led staff to believe there to be a poor future for ONE and its employees.

   Recommendations: Discuss planned changes with employees, and the benefits that will accrue. Allow staff to participate in planning.

Other Issues

The trucking offer should be considered. This offer is based on having other freight on the back haul and thus not returning at cost to ONE. To ensure the best deal, ONE should go to tender. Regardless of who wins the contract, this route is preferable to the present situation of paying for empty trucks on the back haul. Sell the existing trucks, and re-deploy the affected staff.

Conclusion

It is crucial for ONE to proceed immediately with the recommendations. The President should be responsible for their implementation because of their significance to the firm's viability.

## CHAPTER 3

Marking Cases

Understanding how cases are marked clarifies the expectations underlying case analysis, and thereby making it helpful.

There are two basic approaches to marking cases: mechanical and global. Mechanical or analytical marking involves identifying all possible aspects of a perfect answer and assigning a point value to each. This is a thorough, detailed, rigid, and time-consuming approach to case marking. The other method is called global (or holistic) marking (or rating), which takes less time and is less detailed. Global marking involves identifying all important issues. Each response is judged as to how these major issues are addressed. With global marking each paper is generally marked twice. Significant differences between markers must be resolved. The advantage of global marking over mechanical marking is that it is not biased against short, uniquely insightful case responses. The lack of detail is its disadvantage.

Each method is discussed with an example.

MECHANICAL MARKING

As there is no singularly correct answer, mechanical marking must allow for all reasonable perceptions of the issues. To give credence to the expectation of more than one appropriate response, mechanical marking guides must have more marks than the total for the case question. For example, if there are 70 marks for a case question like ONE-BIG FIRM Ltd. in chapter 2, the marking guide could have 124 marks, as noted in this chapter. Seldom do students earn the full marks allotted because of limited time, and because some marks overlap. Thus, any response justified with evidence in the case question will receive marks.

There is another way to explain excess marks. Case questions contain issues or evidence on fundamental or root issues. However, the linkage between an issue and a root issue is not explicit. Students must argue the relationship. For example, in the case response in chapter 2, the root issue

is "current marketing strategy is inappropriate." This is not in the case question, but evidence in the case supports it, e.g., the once successful central purchasing and warehousing approach is more expensive than what competitors use.

Exhibit 3 displays a mechanical marking guide that contains examples of individual preferences for conceptualizing the root issues. Two of the root issues — number 1, "marketing strategy inappropriate," and number 5, "no strategic plan" — relate to long-term, major decisions on how to carry out the business of ONE. The marking guide includes both to reward the various "right answers."

Whenever students mention issues and root issues, they get rewarded with marks. Their issues and root issues may not line up as shown above. Nevertheless, the mechanical markers seek to reward marks against the most appropriate categories in the guide, and sometimes generously.

Besides issues, analysis, and recommendations, there are marks for format and professionalism. Such rewards should be kept in mind when writing the case response, as a little time may pay handsomely. For example, precede the case response with a memorandum. This should be from the person that the student is role playing, to the person and position to whom the case suggests the student is to report. The memorandum should contain a short paragraph linking the case question required with the attached report. The report itself should have headings, e.g., introduction, issues, analysis, recommendations, and conclusion. When using point form, introduce it with a sentence. There should a logical flow to the report. And there should be no glaring deficiencies with grammar, spelling, and sentence structure.

GLOBAL MARKING

This method of marking starts with a ranking of the most important issues that need to be addressed. Then, each issue receives a point score consistent with the ranking. For each issue, a sin-

EXHIBIT 3: MECHANICAL MARKING GUIDE

			Marks	Sub-total
1.	**Issue**	marketing strategy inappropriate	3	
	Analysis	obsolete	2	
		competition	2	
		too expensive	2	
		rigid, non-responsive	2	
	Recommendation	develop new marketing strategy	2	13
2.	**Issue**	CPW too expensive	3	
	Analysis	costs, 12.7%	2	
		competition, 3.5%	2	
		2% advantage on purchases	2	
		7.2% total disadvantage	2	
	Recommendation	decentralize purchasing	2	
		dismantle CPW	2	
		reduce costs	2	17
3.	**Issue**	underutilized warehouse space	3	
	Analysis	25% vacant	2	
		could ship directly	2	
	Recommendation	sublease	2	
		sell	2	11
4.	**Issue**	surplus staff	3	
	Analysis	poor service from CPW	2	
		additional staff required	2	
		CPW should be responsive	2	
	Recommendation	re-deploy expediting staff	2	
		reduce costs	2	13
5.	**Issue**	no strategic plan	3	
	Analysis	blind pursuit of obsolete strategy	2	
		no preparation for changes	2	
	Recommendation	develop a strategic plan	2	9
6.	**Issue**	little concern for profitability	3	
	Analysis	profits have declined significantly	2	
		unabated	2	
		cost control missed	2	
		cost allocation dispute	2	
	Recommendation	profitability to be emphasized	2	
		develop financial orientation	2	
		develop financial goals	2	
		use financial incentives	2	19
7.	**Issue**	morale is bad	2	
	Analysis	problems have depressed employees	2	
	Recommendation	discuss turn-around	2	
		allow employee participation	2	8
8.	**Other issues**	trucking offer — consider	2	
		back haul	2	
		tender	2	
		sell trucks	2	
		re-deploy employees	2	
		other	10	20
*	**Format**	focus on profit improvement	2	
		logical in sequence	2	
		supported statements and assumptions	2	
		spelling and grammar	4	
		addressed to the president	2	
		general impression	2	14
				124

Student mark/70 (Maximum)

```
┌─────────────────────────────────────────────┐
│                                               │
│      EXHIBIT 4: MARKING GUIDE — GLOBAL        │
│                                               │
│  Issues                                       │
│      1.   New strategy needed          25     │
│      2.   Costs out of control         20     │
│      3.   Financial leadership needed  10     │
│                                               │
│  Focus                                        │
│      4.   Sense of urgency, understanding 10  │
│      5.   Professionalism               5     │
│                                        ──     │
│                                        70     │
│                                               │
└─────────────────────────────────────────────┘
```

gle student score would be awarded based on the identification of the issue and related issues, analysis, and recommendations for resolution. Other factors, such as professionalism and realism, can be scored also.

Global marking places more emphasis on the subjective judgment of the marker. It usually takes a few dozen papers before marking consistency can be established. The use of two markers is recommended to reduce bias. This can be waved in favour of time savings when the marker has substantial experience with the case or the case is uncomplicated.

For the example of ONE, the marking guide for global marking could look like the one shown in Exhibit 4.

CASE WRITING TACTICS

The method of marking should not affect how a student responds to a case question. Mechanical marking might favour students using a "shotgun" approach of putting every possible thing down on the case response. Such an approach usually leads to duplication and not much depth or linkage among the various facets of a case question. It would be a poor examination tactic, as it takes time away from a thorough and systematic approach to the case question. Given the time constraints, students should seek to manage their time by understanding the root issues vis-à-vis the "required." They should emphasize identifying, ana-

lyzing, and resolving those root issues, and, only when time is available, discuss the more tangential issues.

Global marking might favour short, uniquely insightful responses. A well-designed mechanical marking guide should do the same. Seeking short, uniquely insightful responses could be dangerous as such responses usually take substantial sifting through the data to find one that addresses all issues, or at least all root issues. It usually takes less time to address issues individually than in total.

A case response that will yield a passing mark must show depth of analysis. This requires sufficient time spent reading the case question in order to understand the case and its issues. The student then has the evidence pointing to the root issues, and can undertake the analysis and make appropriate recommendations. If insufficient time is spent reading, the student will have a superficial response and be unable to say much about the issues or to recommend solutions. In a timed situation, however, spending too much time reading leaves insufficient time for responding. Consequently, students should set in advance the length of their reading time and stick to it. To be able to do this, a student needs to understand a variety of possible cases, and have a rule for each type. Students should develop their rules that satisfy their own approaches. Two extreme examples follow.

1. For multi-technique cases like ONE, 40 percent of the time could be spent reading and 60 percent spent writing. While reading, the relationships between issues and root issues, analysis, and recommendations emerge. Writing time includes time to refine understanding. More ideas will emerge during the writing stage.

2. For a quantitative, directed case like Precious Metals — case 29 of this selection — the reading time might fall to about 15 percent or even less, as the real issues are blatant.

For the majority of student case responses, the earned marks will be the same under both mechanical and global marking.

CHAPTER 4

A Practice Case

Case analysis is the application of management accounting techniques to practical issues and/or real-life situations. In simple cases, the appropriate techniques and issues are explicit. In more complex cases, the appropriate techniques and issues are harder to ascertain.

This chapter and the casebook seek to develop student skills in doing case analysis. The underlying premise is that instruction, coupled with practice and feedback, will produce understanding of the case approach. A first step is provided by this chapter. It explicitly specifies in advance a management accounting technique to be applied to a case question. Normally, the student must determine the management accounting technique. However, by specifying the technique, this chapter explains how

case questions are viewed from the perspective of a particular management accounting technique in determining issues.

Management Accounting Technique

For the case in this chapter, displayed in Exhibit 5, the management accounting technique will be "feedback information." This technique incorporates the belief that information on operations and employee behaviour will facilitate improvements to future performance. This is an underlying belief with financial and nonfinancial reports.

The case, Computer Sales Division, is to be read, and it is to be assessed from the perspective of feedback information during the reading. This technique implies that feedback is useful and nec-

---

EXHIBIT 5: COMPUTER SALES DIVISION

You were a commissioned sales representative for five years. Although business was competitive, for three of those years, you were the top sales representative for your company.

You thoroughly enjoyed your job. You had substantial independence. You selected the firms you wanted to contact. You determined the sales approach. There were no inhibiting rules or regulations. Your boss did not interfere, but instead bought you lunch every first Monday of the month. You did what you wanted to do because you were the top sales representative.

Fourteen months ago your boss retired, and you received his position as the sales manager, central division. Your subordinates include 24 commissioned sales persons, two order processing clerks, and a secretary/receptionist.

On the first day of your new job you made two commitments. First, you told your new boss, the vice president of sales, that your unit's sales and profits would increase by 20 percent in the next year. Second, you gave the sales staff of your unit five steps that, if followed, would double their sales.

Now you regret those commitments. The first year has transpired. Sales are down 15 percent. Profits are down 25 percent. And rather than doubling sales, sales per sales person are down 10 percent, and three sales representatives have gone with a competitor.

In reflecting over the last year, your comments to the sales representatives keep coming back.

The rules for successful selling are simple. By following my five rules, your personal sales will double and, with our commission structure, so will your gross income. My five rules are as follows:

1. Call all regular customers at least once every two weeks. Ask if they are planning to buy computers, equipment, or software. Emphasize that you would be pleased to provide quotations.

EXHIBIT 5...cont'd

2. New customers are essential for sales growth. Make 25 cold calls each month. Five should become new customers. I get company names from the yellow pages, trade directories, etc. With cold calls, I use the telephone and ask the answering receptionist for the person in charge of computer purchases. This usually leads to a few calls and questions before I reach the person most likely to be able to make purchases from us. I present myself, our company, and the fact that we supply and support IBM compatible equipment and software.

3. I meet my active clients regularly. Clients with sales potential of less than $150,000 are met once a year. See clients twice a year if they have more potential.

4. Every month I send each active client something in the mail or through e-mail that keeps them aware of my name and telephone number.

5. I return all calls within an hour. This requires an answering service (no voice mail), a cellular telephone, and a beeper.

With these steps I can work independently and effectively. I meet only once every month for lunch with my boss and all he does is to keep me informed about our new products.

These five steps have come to haunt you. All sales representatives have adamantly said they followed the five steps. They blame you for their failures. You do not know if they are telling the truth, or if they are not following the steps, or if the procedures are not effective for all sales representatives.

Very concerned with the decline in sales, the vice-president reviewed the five steps and admitted their validity. However, he suggested that they may not represent all the steps for successful selling. As an example, he mentioned that the content of discussions with clients and methods for closing a sale are important, but not included in the five steps. He also informed you that there have been complaints about sales representatives who compete with one another for the same orders.

You are confused. You know how to sell, but you do not know if your sales representatives know how.

Required

Using the case approach and the feedback information perspective, identify the root issues, analyze them, and make recommendations for resolving the issues.

essary if management is to be successful in directing employees. Consequently, the lack of feedback means that management is less than opti- mal, and problems have occurred or will occur because of the lack of feedback.

CHAPTER 5

Analyzing Activities

A current trend in management accounting textbooks is to focus on activities. The activities that form costs are the concern, not resultant dollars per se. Managers need to manage activities to influence product and service costs.

The management of activities has long been associated with scientific management and Frederick Taylor (1911), an early and vocal proponent. More recently, Michael Porter (1980, 1985) has supported the activity focus. He argues that the value of a product or service in the eyes of consumers is a result of activities. Keep the activities that add value, discard the others.

This chapter of the book encourages students to venture into non-manufacturing organizations—service, trade, government, and nonprofit—to study and apply management accounting at the activity level. A general framework provides assistance to the venture. Real organizations are to be chosen, but students are not to select an entire organization. They should examine some meaningful but distinct part. Ideally there will be seven to twelve employees with three or four different position classifications. The requirement is for depth of analysis and not broad and superficial coverage.

Students are to work together in groups of two to four, and they must prepare a proposal. The proposal, about one page, should identify the organization, unit, number of employees and positions, and discuss the project steps. Approval of the proposal by the instructor is mandatory. Results of the project are to be written up in a formal report with introduction and conclusion—a recommended length of 12 to 15 pages, plus appendices. The following list contains the steps:

1. **Describe the organization and unit**. This section should be brief, but emphasis should be placed on what is important to the organization and how the unit contributes to the achievement of organizational objectives.

2. **List all activities**. In fulfilling the requirements of a position an employee undertakes many activities. Students are to aggregate the activities of each classification into a few activities, probably four to eight significant ones. Describe the relationship between activities and positions with flow diagrams. (This technique is described in Exhibit 6.) Use a matrix to show the activities associated with each position. The matrix will simplify scheduling and suggest where cross training will increase flexibility in scheduling the accomplishment of the unit's responsibilities.

   The emphasis should be on actual activities that drive costs—such as taking an order, processing an invoice and changing four tires—and not responsibilities. For some, especially senior positions, activities will be difficult to document. A block of time may be the best means of assigning time, e.g., a supervisor's time for recruitment.

3. **Conduct observations**. Students are to observe and time employees undertaking activities. Through these observations, establish work-to-time relationships; i.e., figure out the time required to complete each activity. This will tend to be an average time, and there will be a variance around the average.

4. **Identify activity changes**. From observations or analysis, students are to develop better methods for performing some activities, i.e., reduce costs, increase value. Students should consider changes to work flow, work methods, procedures, etc. that will allow activities to be streamlined and done in less time.

5. **Establish standards**. Based on observations and in consultation with the unit's manager and employees, choose reasonable time standards for performing each activity. Incorporate the required level of service or quality in the standard. A standard is not necessarily an average. It is a reasonable goal for a good employee working at a reasonable rate.

6. **Gather activity driver data**. To assign employees to work, it is first necessary to gather historical data on activity drivers, by time of year, week, or day, etc. An activity driver is an event associated with the activity that results in the consumption of the organization's resources. For example, a fast food restaurant has a dominant activity driver in the number of orders. With more orders, crew members have more activities for serving customers, preparing food, and delivering food. Some activities are without activity drivers. Assign blocks of time for those activities, e.g., allocate one hour a day to the manager for scheduling employees at a fast food restaurant. If actual data are not available, consult the unit's manager and employees for estimates. These data should result in workable, simple, and meaningful activity driver models showing differences during the year, week, or day. Remember, it is the activity driver that leads to the need for activities.

7. **Determine employee hour requirements**. Using the above models for activity drivers and the established standards, calculate the number of employee hours to accomplish the requisite activities individually and in total. A simplified example would be where the activity driver is the number of customers, and where the model specifies 150 clients a day. With, say, 10 activities to serve a client totalling 16 minutes, the need is for 2,400 minutes (150 × 16) or 40 hours of employee time. Typically, models would be more complicated, and the employee hour requirements differ by time of year, week, or day.

8. **Schedule employees**. Make suggestions for the scheduling of employees for effectively and efficiently accomplishing the unit's activities while adding value. Recognize that employees cannot work at 100 percent utilization. Employees frequently and legally have work (i.e., coffee) breaks. Moreover, employees

---

EXHIBIT 6: STRUCTURED SYSTEMS ANALYSIS

This flow diagramming technique describes business activities for formulating computer applications. It is also effective in business improvement studies. Structured systems analysis (SSA) works on the idea that a picture (or a diagram) is worth a multitude of words. The inherent clarity of a diagram is not easily replicated in words alone.

For the management accountant, SSA has two advantages. First, it enhances the understanding of the activities within an organizational unit. It concentrates on detailed activities. These activities comprise the basis of responsibilities for aggregate revenues and costs. This allows questioning of what is being done (e.g., is an activity really necessary), how the activity is being done (e.g., are there means for increasing efficiency and/or effectiveness), and what the reasonable time is for accomplishing an activity. This enhanced understanding allows management accountants to better identify opportunities for improvement. The second advantage is that SSA allows the management accountant to develop or assist in the development of an information system based on insightful and controllable activities.

There are only five symbols for diagramming with SSA. SSA's graphic language provides a versatile vehicle for understanding an organizational unit at the activity and sub-activity level. The symbols are described below. The example on page 20 illustrates an application of the symbols to an organizational unit from a provincial social services department.

Symbols

Activities:
- Process identification
- Descriptive name
- Position performing activity

External Entities:
- Source or destination for activities/ data, i.e., anything outside the particular set of activities
- Duplication symbol

Storage of data regarding activities

Data or information flow

Activity flow

REFERENCES

Mendes, K.S., "Structured Systems Analysis: A Technique to Define Business Requirements," Sloan Management Review, Summer 1980, pp. 51–63.

Ozerkevich, M.J., and G.P. Spraakman, "Adding Rigor to Management: A Case Study of Structured Systems Analysis," *Optimum*, 1987, No. 2, pp. 22–37.

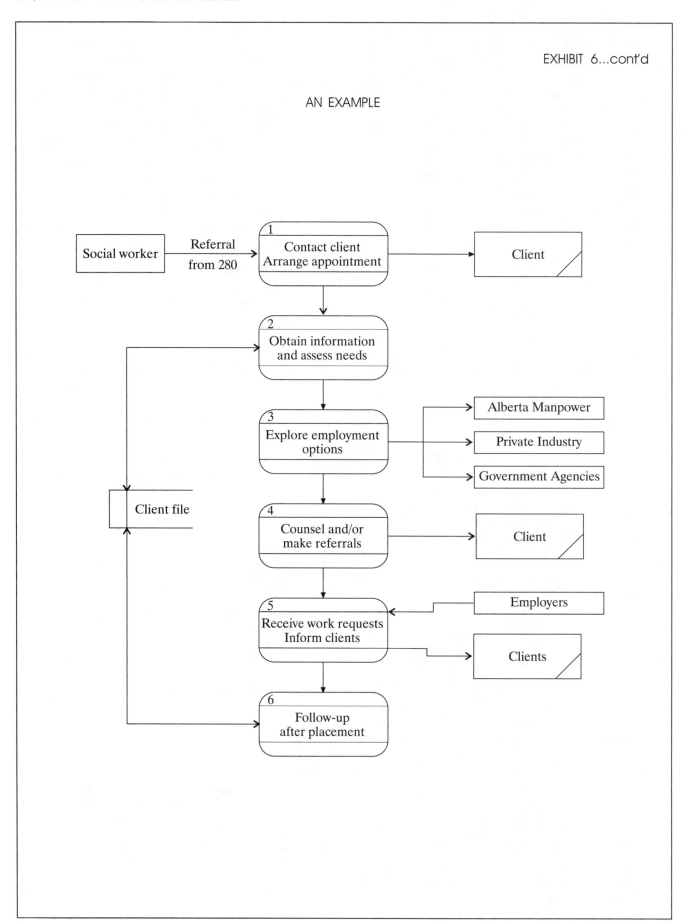

EXHIBIT 6...cont'd

AN EXAMPLE

make personal telephone calls and engage in social (non-organizational) talk, without threat or loss of their jobs. Thus, employees do not work 100 percent of the time, but 85 percent or 90 percent of the time after deducting coffee breaks. The important goal is the accomplishment of a unit's required activities, while maintaining the target utilization rate. Employee hour requirements suggest part-time employees for peak activity levels instead of full-time employees who would be underused during slow activity periods.

9. **Develop an information system**. With the understanding of how activities get accomplished, develop a feedforward and feedback system for managing employees. This should start with activity drivers expectations for a year, week, or day. Then schedule the number of employees needed to meet this volume of activity drivers. The standard time per activity and the utilization rate directly influence the number of employees required. An informa-

tion system would compare these expectations with the actual activity driver volumes, scheduled employees, and utilization rates. It would suggest the appropriateness of the standards. In many ways this would be a flexible budget, complete with actual results and variance analysis, but at the level of activities instead of dollars. This system should be simple and explicit. It should add value in the eyes of the customer.

Examples of analyzing activities are displayed in Appendices 1 and 2. These examples display complete applications.

REFERENCES

Porter, M.E., *Competitive Strategy* (New York, NY: Free Press, 1980).

———, *Competitive Advantage* (New York, NY: Free Press, 1985).

Taylor, F.W., *The Principles of Scientific Management* (New York, NY: Harper & Brothers, 1911).

Benevolent and Research Society

The mission of the Benevolent and Research Society is to eradicate a certain prevalent disease and in the meantime enhance the quality of life for people living with it. This is done by delivering educational and patient programs, and by participating in research, fundraising and advocacy. Volunteers and paid employees share these responsibilities.

The Society has a national office and 10 divisions across Canada. Substantial importance is placed on research co-ordinated by the national research institute, which receives 48 percent of the revenues. These revenues come from public fundraising. None comes from government organizations.

The subject division has 54 employees. Employees and volunteers at this office co-ordinate provincial activities, prepare and develop programs for use by the districts, units, and branches. This project focuses on the activities of the eight employees in the division's accounting department, which also provides accounting services for the districts and units. The department is vital to the continued operation of the organization because it processes accounts receivable, accounts payable, cheques, etc. and produces current, accurate financial information. This information assists all levels of the division to plan, control, and make decisions.

POSITIONS AND ACTIVITIES

Listed below are the positions in the accounting department and some major duties assigned to each.

Accounting Supervisor

- Hires, trains, supervises, motivates, and evaluates departmental staff

- Oversees the operation of the accounts payable and revenue sections
- Prepares monthly financial statements
- Reviews, verifies, and co-ordinates the preparation of budgets across the province
- Ensures funds are invested in approved financial institutions at high yields
- Checks authorizations on all requests for payment
- Works with the auditors to ensure an accurate and efficient external audit
- Verifies all transactions before entering into the general ledger

Assistant Accounting Supervisor

- Reconciles cash accounts and bank statements for the units against the division's ledger
- Monitors and provides day-to-day direction to the other accounting staff and accounting support to staff in district and unit offices
- Analyzes various accounts on the computer and provides written reports as required
- Maintains and posts the designated bequest ledger monthly, encodes and checks accuracy of account numbers
- Reviews and redirects daily mail
- Obtains investment rates and makes investments

Senior Accounting Clerk

- Prepares monthly bank reconciliations for the general transfer accounts, units' working funds, and transfer accounts
- Reconciles the unit and branch imprest, petty cash, employee, temporary, and unit advances with the general ledger

Adapted from a case by Paul Ahima, Michael Appiah, Mark Dalrymple, Yvonne Cheng, Manjit Rai, Paulett Ramsey and Sonia Shkolnik.

- Records daily the revenue reports and bank statements for all units
- Maintains petty cash float at specified levels
- Records the mileage and gas used, and prepares annual gas tax rebate submission forms
- Prepares reports, conducts account analysis, acts as backup to assistant accounting supervisor and in-memorial-receipts clerk

Senior Accounts Payable Clerk

- Verifies accuracy of vendor invoices and reconciles them with monthly statements
- Codes and keys in invoices for payment, produces cheques and the cheque register bi-weekly
- Responds to suppliers' and units' queries and maintains up-to-date vendor files
- Obtains signatures on cheques, mails or distributes cheques
- Relieves receptionist

Junior Accounts Payable Clerk

- Records receipts of units' reimbursement claims, verifies vouchers to cheque copies, assigns accounts to various charges; checks for adjustments to the working fund from bank reconciliation
- Checks unit reimbursements to ensure adherence to policy and accuracy of account numbers
- Keys invoices, unit reimbursements into the computer for the production of cheques
- Separates cheques, sends to payees, sorts and files copies
- Annually removes appropriate files for microfilming or storing and prepares files for next fiscal year
- Relieves receptionist

In-Memorial-Receipts Clerk

- Receives and verifies balanced daily control sheets itemizing details, cheques and cash from assistant accounting supervisor; classifies and credits funds to appropriate accounts
- Prepares deposit slips and makes daily deposits
- Issues and sends donations and bequest receipts and in-memorial cards
- Prepares accounts receivable invoices upon request
- Receives and processes patient transportation reimbursement claims for all units

- Types correspondence and bequest statement
- Relieves receptionist

Data Entry Clerk

- Keys in all transactions to the general ledger
- Collates and prepares monthly statements to all units
- Files source documents
- Maintains the receipt book control sheets by assigning receipt book numbers to units and updating same
- Keys in annual budgets for all departments, districts and units

Receptionist

- Provides empathetic and courteous telephone and reception services to callers and visitors
- Arranges for taxis and limousine services
- Provides word processing for the accounting supervisor
- Enters imprest reimbursements into the computer
- Verifies outgoing cheques

Instead of listing activities by employee, the following schedule groups common activities.

1. Hires, motivates and evaluates departmental staff

2. Trains, supervises and oversees employees' daily activities
   - oversees daily activities of department
   - checks invoices and outgoing cheques
   - checks investment vehicles
   - checks petty cash transactions

3. Processes invoices and reimbursement claims
   - receives invoices and reimbursement claims
   - sends to appropriate department for authorization
   - codes invoices
   - keys in data

4. Prepares cheques from computerized information
   - issues cheques
   - attaches backup information to cheques
   - checks the accuracy of the cheques
   - obtains signatures on cheques
   - separates, sorts and files cheque copies
   - forwards cheques to payees or requisitioner

5. Processing revenues
   - receives donations, bequests, and in-memorial revenues

EXHIBIT A

	AS	AAS	SAC	SAPC	JAPC	IMRC	DEC	R
Training and supervising	X	X		X				
Processing invoices and reimbursement claims				X	X	X		
Prepares cheques	X	X		X	X	X	X	X
Prepares monthly financial statements	X	X	X	X	X	X	X	X
Co-ordination and re-distribution of budgets	X						X	
Telephone and reception services				X	X	X	X	
Accounts receivable invoices	X				X			
Processing revenues and making deposits		X	X			X		
Obtains investment rates and makes investments	X	X						
Reconciles all accounts	X	X	X	X				
General ledger entries		X	X	X				

Note: AS — accounting supervisor; AAS — assistant accounting supervisor; SAC — senior accounting clerk; SAPC — senior accounts payable clerk; JAPC — junior accounts payable clerk; IMRC — in-memorial-receipts clerk, DEC — data entry clerk; and R — receptionist.

* prepares deposit list
* checks deposit list
* makes deposit

6. Reconciliation of accounts
   * keys in all revenues to general ledger
   * reconciles cash flow and bank statements
   * reconciles working fund and transfer accounts
   * reconciles various advances and petty cash float

7. Prepares accounts receivable invoices
   * receives request to issue invoice for patient transportation, overpayment of expense claims or non-chargeable expenses
   * codes and inputs data into the computer
   * prints invoices
   * verifies accuracy and mails invoices

8. Budgeting
   * prepares budget forms
   * submits to division, districts and units
   * reviews and verifies budget submissions
   * keys in budget data
   * prints and distributes individual budgets

9. Reception
   * responds to incoming telephone calls and greets visitors

* provides word processing services to supervisor
* arranges for taxi and limousine services

ACTIVITY MATRIX

The matrix in Exhibit A displays the relationship between major activities and positions in the accounting department.

Cross training and scheduling are not obvious in the lists of major duties. However, there is a system in place under which employees can do more than their own jobs to ensure ongoing activities during periods of vacation or illness.

OBSERVATIONS

Observations and interviews determined the actual time spent on each activity. The table in Exhibit B shows these times.

ACTIVITY CHANGES

Volunteers perform many activities at the districts and units. One activity change would be to have district and unit staff check, approve, and accept responsibility for all reports, invoices, purchase orders, expense claims, budgets, and reimbursement

EXHIBIT B

Activities	Actual Time Requirements	
Supervising	5	minutes an employee a day
Obtains investment rates	5	minutes a telephone call (3 calls per investment)
Makes investment	10	minutes per investment
Issues petty cash	2	minutes per issue
Checks an invoice	1	minutes per invoice
Sends invoice for authorization	0.5	minutes per invoice
Manually codes invoice	0.25	minutes per invoice
Keys in cheque information	1.5	minutes per invoice
Manually types comments on cheque	1	minute per cheque
Matches cheque with invoice	30	seconds per invoice
Separates cheques	15	seconds per cheque
Files cheque copy	15	seconds per cheque copy
Checks unit reimbursement claim	5	minutes per claim
Prepares daily deposit list	2	hours per list
Makes deposit at bank	1	hour per deposit
Types receipt/in-memorial card	5	minutes per receipt/card
Keys in transaction to general ledger	2	minutes per transaction
Reconciles cash	45	minutes a reconciliation
Reconciles bank statement	45	minutes per statement
Prepares monthly financial statement	30	hours per month
Keys in budget data	10	minutes per budget
Distributes individual budget	1	minute per budget
Prepares annual audited financial statements	60	hours per year
Responds to incoming telephone calls	0.5	minute per call

claims. This checking would reduce errors and save time: approximately 0.12 seconds per invoice and a 20 percent decrease for checking reports, purchase orders, expense claims, budgets, and reimbursement claims.

A second change would be to purchase minor computer software to list outstanding cheques at the end of the month. Specifically, these changes would allow the printing of receipts, cards, and comment lines on cheques. The savings would be five hours a month for bank statement reconciliations, one minute per cheque, and approximately two minutes per receipt or card.

Third, send mail directly from the mailroom to the incurring department for authorization and general ledger account coding. Then submit to the accounting department for payment. This would save 0.5 minutes per invoice.

ESTABLISH STANDARDS

The accounting department has the following response standards:

- respond to inquiries within two days,
- pay suppliers within 14 days or 30 days (decided by distance from the division office),
- reimburse units within 14 days, and
- make daily deposits by 3:00 p.m.

With these response standards, time-to-complete-an-activity standards were developed (see Exhibit C).

The standards for the other activities remain at the observed rates.

ACTIVITY DRIVERS

Historical volume data with differences during the day, week and year were not readily available. Thus, the team questioned each member of the department regarding cyclical patterns during the day, week, month and year. Although activities levels did vary, there were opportunities to smooth or manage these fluctuations.

Notable increases in workload occur during the April campaign, where the accounting department

EXHIBIT C

Activities	Standard Time Requirements	
Matches cheque with invoice	25	seconds per invoice
Separates cheques	10	seconds per cheque
Files cheque copy	10	seconds per cheque copy
Checks unit reimbursement claim	3.5	minutes per claim
Prepares daily deposit list	1.5	hours per list
Types receipt or in-memorial card	4	minutes per receipt/card
Keys in transaction to general ledger	1.5	minutes a transaction
Reconciles cash flow	30	minutes per unit reconciliation
Reconciles bank statement	30	minutes per statement
Prepares monthly financial statements	27	hours per month
Keys in budget data	8	minutes per budget
Distributes individual budget	1	minute per budget
Prepares annual audited financial statements	55	hours per year

EXHIBIT D

Activities	Regular Volume		Campaign Volume	
Invoices, expense claims processed	40	per day	40	per day
Cheques	130	per week	130	per week
Receipts	20	per day	25	per day
In memorial cards	10	per day	13	per day
Data entries to general ledger	750	per day	937	per day
Incoming cheques per deposit	25	per day	31	per day
Incoming telephone calls	400	per day	500	per day
Co-ordinate budgets	140	per year	140	per year

experiences an approximately 25 percent increase in the number of donations. Exhibit D illustrates the increases, which can be managed by smoothing or shifting the work to later time periods.

EMPLOYEE HOUR REQUIREMENTS

Exhibit E identifies the volume of the activity driver per average day, the standard time for the activity, and their product the required employee time per activity. Accumulating by position and comparing to the available employee time per day yields the utilization rate.

Utilization specifies the proportion of occupied employee hours if he or she accomplishes the activities within the established time standards. A full working day contains eight working hours. That time decreases by 15 percent for lunches and other breaks. Expected total hours available for work are 6.8 hours per employee. This would be 100 percent utilization, but 85 to 90 percent would be a more reasonable expectation.

SCHEDULING EMPLOYEES

The utilization rates suggest eliminating the assistant accounting supervisor and junior accounts payable clerk positions, and reassign their activities to other positions.

The assistant accounting supervisor and junior accounts payable clerk work at utilization rates of 43 percent and 51 percent, respectively. The activities of the first position overlap those of the accounting supervisor and senior accounting clerk.

EXHIBIT E: EMPLOYEE HOUR REQUIREMENTS

	Volume	Standard Time		Per Day Required Employee Minutes
Accounting Supervisor				
Hires, trains (yearly)	1	15	hours	4
Oversees the operation of accounts payable and revenue sections minutes per day per employee	7	5	minutes	35
Prepares monthly financial statements (monthly)	1	27	hours	81
Reviews and co-ordinates all budgets (yearly)	1	68	hours	17
Makes investments (daily)	2	5	minutes	10
Checks authorizations on all requests for payment (daily)	40	1	minute	40
Works with the auditors (yearly)	1	55	hours	14
Verifies transactions (daily)	1	30	minutes	30
Utilization rate, 56%				230
Assistant Accounting Supervisor				
Reconciles bank statements (monthly)	60	30	minutes	90
Monitors and provides day-to-day accounting direction (daily)	7	5	minutes	35
Analyzes accounts (daily)	2	5	minutes	10
Maintains and posts designated bequest ledger monthly, codes and checks account numbers (monthly)	40	5	minutes	10
Reviews and redirects mail (daily)	20	1	minute	20
Makes investments (daily)	2	5	minutes	10
Utilization rate, 43%				175
Senior Accounting Clerk				
Reconciles bank statements (monthly)	60	30	minutes	90
Reconciles other accounts with general ledger (monthly)	60	30	minutes	90
Records transactions (monthly)	60	30	minutes	90
Maintains petty cash float (daily)	2	2	minutes	4
Records the mileage and gas (monthly)	20	5	minutes	5
Prepares reports and conducts account analysis, backup to assistant accounting supervisor and in-memorial-receipts clerk (daily)	1	10	minutes	10
Utilization rate, 71%				289
Senior Accounts Payable Clerk				
Verifies vendor invoices, reconciles with monthly statements (daily)	40	1	minute	40
Codes, keys in invoices for payment, produces cheques and cheque register (daily)	26	5	minutes	130
Responds to queries and maintains vendor files (daily)	10	2	minutes	20
Obtains signatures on cheques, mails or distributes cheques (daily)	26	2	minutes	52
Relieves receptionist (daily)	1	30	minutes	30
Utilization rate, 67%				272
Junior Accounts Payable Clerk				
Records unit reimbursement claims, assigns accounts and checks working fund accounts (daily)	6	5	minutes	30
Checks unit reimbursements for adherence to policy (daily)	6	5	minutes	30
Keys in invoices, unit reimbursements (daily)	60	1	minute	60
Prepares cheques for distribution and files copies (daily)	26	1	minute	26
Replace files, microfilming (daily)	1	6	minutes	6
Relieves receptionist (daily)	1	60	minutes	60
Utilization rate, 51%				212

EXHIBIT E...cont'd

	Volume	Standard Time	Per Day Required Employee Minutes
In-Memorial-Receipts Clerk			
Receives and verifies balanced daily control sheets, classifies, credits funds to accounts, prepares deposit slips, and makes deposits (daily)	1	180 minutes	180
Issues donation and bequest receipts and in-memorial cards (weekly)	30	4 minutes	120
Prepares accounts receivable invoices (daily)	2	5 minutes	10
Receives, processes patient transportation reimbursement claims for units (daily)	6	3 minutes	18
Types correspondence (daily)	1	30 minutes	30
Relieves receptionist (daily)	1	30 minutes	30
Utilization rate, 95%			388
Data Entry Clerk			
Keys in transactions to general ledger (daily)	200	1.5 minutes	300
Collates monthly statements (daily)	6	0.5 minutes	3
Files source documents (daily)	30	0.5 minutes	15
Maintains the receipt book control sheets by assigning receipt book numbers to units, updating (daily)	2	2.5 minutes	5
Keys in annual budgets (yearly)	140	10 minutes	6
Utilization rate, 81%			329
Receptionist			
Provides telephone and reception services to callers, visitors (daily)	400	0.5 minutes	200
Arranges for taxis and limousines (daily)	2	2 minutes	4
Provides word processing services (daily)	1	60 minutes	60
Enters imprest reimbursements (daily)	6	5 minutes	30
Verifies outgoing cheques (daily)	26	1 minute	26
Utilization rate, 78%			320

The senior accounting clerk could undertake the first position's bank reconciliation and account analysis activities. Moreover, the accounting supervisor and the assistant accounting supervisor could provide the day-to-day accounting direction to districts and units. Account number coding and accuracy checking are part of the duties of the senior accounts payable clerk. The receptionist can redirect daily mail. Also, the senior accounts payable clerk should post and maintain the bequest ledger.

The junior accounts payable clerk's activities can be distributed as follows:

• Verify unit reimbursements — senior accounts payable clerk

• Input invoices and reimbursements — senior accounts payable clerk, data entry clerk and/or receptionist

• Run cheques, verify and type comments from adjustment book — senior accounts payable clerk

• Filing and annual file changeover — senior accounts clerk or data entry clerk

The elimination of these positions will result in cost savings and the removal of the friction that comes from ill-defined and overlapping positions.

INFORMATION SYSTEM

On an annual, monthly, and daily basis, an information system would include expected volumes for activity drivers, such as number of invoices, cheques issued, budgets prepared, etc. The occupants of the positions have responsibility for accomplishing the volumes, along with the time standards for accomplishing each activity. There would also be a targeted utilization rate with these assignments. This part of the information system is similar to a budget. However, instead of dollar amounts, it would be in terms of expected number of activities to be done and standard times per activity.

Actual volumes for activity drivers would be compared to expected volumes, and variances would be analyzed. The learning from the feedback would help in maintaining currently attainable standards and accuracy in forecasting activity driver volumes.

APPENDIX 2

Blackjack

Blackjack is a gambling game offered by a casino along with wheel of fortune and roulette. The casino operates during the 10 days of a city's annual exhibition. The casino distributes profits among charitable organizations. Readers unfamiliar with blackjack may want to consult Exhibit F.

The blackjack operation consists of five positions as noted in the following diagram. This study's concern is with the dealers.

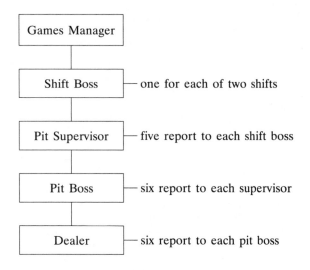

```
┌─────────────────┐
│ Games Manager   │
└─────────────────┘
         │
┌─────────────────┐
│ Shift Boss      │── one for each of two shifts
└─────────────────┘
         │
┌─────────────────┐
│ Pit Supervisor  │── five report to each shift boss
└─────────────────┘
         │
┌─────────────────┐
│ Pit Boss        │── six report to each supervisor
└─────────────────┘
         │
┌─────────────────┐
│ Dealer          │── six report to each pit boss
└─────────────────┘
```

A games manager is responsible for blackjack and the other two games. There is one shift boss for each of the two shifts (10 a.m. to 6 p.m. and 6 p.m. to 2 a.m.). Each pit supervisor is responsible for six pit bosses, and each pit boss supervises all activities, players, and dealers at six tables. Dealers are responsible for their immediate table.

Each dealer works an eight-hour shift. After an hour of work, there is a 15-minute break. Thus, a pit of 30 tables requires 36 dealers. A dealer's responsibilities include selling chips to players for cash, monitoring player activity for unlawful behaviour, making no assumptions on players' hands,

ensuring players' intentions to either hit or pass are made clearly, and reporting any irregularities or errors to the pit boss.

Activities

Dealer activities can be classified into two groups: direct and indirect. Direct activities consist of dealing the cards, shuffling the cards, and exchanging money and chips. Dealing the cards is the actual playing of the game. Exhibit F describes these activities. The actions involved are dealing out the cards, paying out winnings, and collecting lost bets. Shuffling the cards consists of the dealer calling out "shuffle up" to the pit boss and pausing briefly for acknowledgment. The dealer then mixes the cards using a series of well-defined movements. A final direct activity is that of making change. Here the dealer accepts money in exchange for chips or for an equal amount in different denominations.

Indirect activities are non-essential to blackjack, but they enhance the flow of the game. The activities include organizing the chip tray, conversing, and changing shifts. The first is done to make money changing smoother and quicker. Conversing can be broken down into two types: to enhance customer relations, and to answer questions and explain the game. As for breaks, they are vital for maintaining dealer performance and customer satisfaction. Exhibit G shows these activities.

Dealer activities had few opportunities for improvement. There are, however, opportunities to improve the matching of dealers with players. The differences in skills place a dealer in one of three categories:

Neophyte: They started training only two months before the casino opened. The games manager estimated that 30 percent of the dealers were of this type.

Adapted from a case by J. Herschmiller, B. Wong and W. Yung.

EXHIBIT F: BLACKJACK RULES OF PLAY

General Description

Blackjack is a card game, played with a pack of four standard decks dealt from a shoe by a dealer, in which up to seven players participate. Only the dealer may touch the cards, which he plays face up.

Object of Game

Each player attempts to achieve a higher total point value per hand than the dealer, without exceeding a value of 21. If a point count exceeds 21, the hand has "busted," and the bet is automatically lost. If the player's and dealer's point totals are equal, this is a "push" (stand-off) and nobody wins or loses.

Point Value of Cards

There are rules for counting points:

- Aces count "1" or "11," at the player's election. Face cards count "10," and all other cards represent their face value. Card suits do not count.
- A "soft" hand is one that contains an ace counted as 11. All other hands are "hard" in point value. A "hard" hand contains no aces, or the aces are counted as "1."

Natural or Blackjack

If the first two cards dealt to a player total 21, this is a "natural" or "Blackjack" and takes precedence over any three-or-more card point total of 21. If player and dealer have a Blackjack, it is a "push."

Player Options

Each player receives one card, then the dealer takes one card. The players then receive a second card, after which each player has the following options:

- *Hit:* Receives an additional card (a blackjack cannot be hit). To obtain the card, the player makes a beckoning motion with his hand. After each "hit" the player may continue to hit as many cards as he wishes until his/her point count reaches or exceeds 21.
- *Stand:* Receive no additional cards. The player signals the dealer by waving his hand, open palm down. Players use only hand signals. Dealers will not accept verbal decisions.
- *Double down:* If the first two cards dealt total 10 or 11, the player can place an additional, separate bet equal to the original. It is placed in the square. Then one additional card is received. A player may not double down on a blackjack. If the dealer makes a blackjack, the player loses only the original bet.
- *Pair splitting:* If the first two cards are of equal point value, each becomes a separate hand by placing an additional, separate bet equal to the original. It is placed on the outside lines. Only split aces are limited to one additional card per hand. The player plays one hand before the other. If the dealer makes a blackjack, the player loses only the original bet. A two-card 21 on a split hand is not a blackjack for the purposes of a payoff. When splitting any pair, no more than two hands may develop from the original two cards.

Betting and Limits

There are rules for betting.

- Betting is done only with chips purchased from a dealer.
- Chips of different value have different colours. The chip value and colour of each denomination are noted as follows:

$ 0.50	bronze
$ 1.00	red
$ 5.00	black
$ 25.00	blue and yellow
$100.00	brown, red, and gold

- The dealer's chip tray is arranged, going from left to right in the following sequence: $0.50, $1.00, $5.00, $25.00, $100.00.
- Bets are valid only when put upon the space provided on the table before dealing commences. They remain unchanged during play (unless splitting or doubling down). Chips outside the betting square are not considered bets.

- Unalterable betting limits shall be

$2–$50 Tables	=	one hand	$2–50	
		two hands	$20–50	per hand
		three hands	$50	per hand
$5–$100 Tables	=	one hand	$5–100	
		two hands	$40–100	per hand
		three hands	$100	per hand

- Bets shall be of $1 multiples.
- Players shall not play, or exercise any form of control over, more than three betting spaces.

Pay-offs

Players with blackjacks get paid at three to two; other winning hands get paid at one to one.

Sequence of Play

There are some basic steps to blackjack:

1. *Cards*. The dealer deals cards from a pack of 208 new cards (four decks). They are "ribbon" spread on the table for front and back examination by the dealer. There are no jokers. They remain ribbon spread, face up, until play commences. Shuffling is always done twice.

   Dealers change cards at the shuffle. Pit bosses remove used cards from the table. Simultaneously they check for flaws, bind the cards with a rubber band, and record with an attached note the date, time of day and game number. The pit boss signs a note certifying that cards are free of flaws, or shall report flaws immediately to the games manager. The same procedure applies at the close of the final day.

   If the game is temporarily closed and the dealer is relieved without replacement, the pit boss removes the shoe and cards for safekeeping. If all players leave, the dealer combines the cards from the shoe with discards, ribbon spreads them face-up on the table, awaiting commencement of play. The general manager collects all cards at the final day closing. He retains them for at least seven days.

2. *Shuffle, cut, or stop card*. Before play commences, the dealer thoroughly shuffles the cards, and calls to the pit boss, "Shuffle up," and pauses briefly for acknowledgment. The dealer uses only the table ribbon-shuffle, with all cards face down and none exposed to anyone.

   To start, the dealer moves the pack forward on the table and cuts it into two approximate halves. Then the dealer cuts each to make four similarly sized piles of cards. The piles are then shuffled according to a standard procedure.

   After shuffling, the dealer squares the centre pile of all four decks. A player cuts by inserting a cut-card. The player's card must be at least one deck deep. If it should occur that no player wants to make the cut, the dealer cuts. The dealer then places the front section of the cut pack, with the cut-card, behind the rest of pack. Next, the dealer squares the cards against the shoe and inserts the cut-card 35 to 55 cards from bottom of pack before placing the cards in the shoe. After placing in the shoe, the first card is kept face down, i.e., "burned." Burning is the placement of a card face down in the discard holder. The dealer does not show the burned card.

   When the stop-card appears during play, the dealer shuffles the pack after completing the current rough, no matter the number of cards left in the shoe. Then the dealer removes the remaining cards in the shoe, and places them in front of the chip tray for reshuffling.

3. *Basic play*. The deal begins when all players have made their wagers within the betting squares. The dealer runs his hand over the table from right to left to check all bets.

   Starting on the left, the dealer gives each player one card face up. The dealer also takes one face-up card. Then the dealer gives the players a second face-up card. Players receive hits by a hand signal (motion towards themselves). Similarly, players show their intentions to not take a hit with hand signals (motion away from themselves).

4. *Change-ins*. Dealers do not accept cash or chips from players by hand. Players place chips on the table for pickup by dealer.

   Dealers call out all colour and money changes by stating the amount.

5. *Tray management*. Dealers keep their trays neat, especially before shuffling.

6. *Fills*. As a tray gets low on chips, the pit boss orders the dealer a fill. This is a tray of chips totalling $3,575, of a distinctive chip arrangement. Both the dealer and the pit boss will check the amount and sign a statement confirming it.

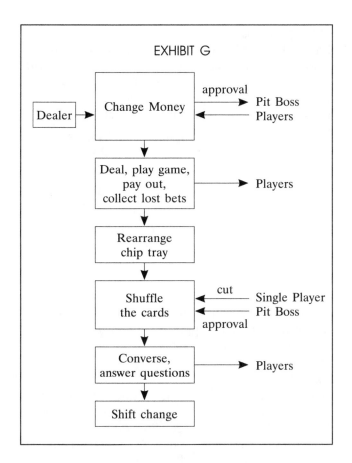

EXHIBIT G

Intermediate: These were dealers who had dealt at a regular casino within the last year. Many of these dealers were neophytes last year. About 30 percent of the dealers were intermediates.

Expert: These dealers were full-time blackjack dealers for longer than 18 months. About 40 percent of the dealers were experts.

Similarly, according to their skill and likelihood to spend money, players were categorized into three types:

Fun-Seeker: These players typically are there for the exhibition and merely want to try gambling. They are often first-timers and usually stay about two hours. They usually play conservatively and will lose $20 each on average.

Rambo: They know how to play blackjack and come for recreation. These players do not care if they lose. They come for fun. Rambos stay for about four hours and tend to lose about $200 per sitting.

Regular: These persons, mostly retired, appear daily at casinos. Regulars tend to stay "rooted" for approximately eight hours on average and lose about $30 each time.

The above data on player categories and spending can be explained in terms of money spent per hour:

	Time Spent	Money Spent	Money Spent per Hour
Fun-Seeker	2 hrs	$ 20.00	$10.00
Rambo	4 hrs	200.00	50.00
Regular	8 hrs	30.00	3.75

The pit boss divides the tables into two types: high limit ($5 to $100 bets), and low limit ($2 to $50 bets). The games manager estimated the relative proportion of the three types of players at both the high- and low-limit tables to be as follows:

	High-Limit Table	Low-Limit Table
Fun-Seeker	1	2
Rambo	5	2
Regular	1	3

Note, full tables have seven players.

There are about 41 rounds per hour of dealing. A round is completed when the dealer deals a complete game to each player. The following shows what each type of player loses after each hand, with the amount of money spent in an hour converted into the amount spent in a round:

	Spent Per Hour	Spent Per Round
Fun-Seeker	$10.00	$0.24
Rambo	50.00	1.22
Regular	3.75	0.09

The above numbers are then used to construct an expected revenue schedule, as shown below. It considers the number and type of players at each table.

	High-Limit Table		Low-Limit Table	
Fun-Seeker	0.24	(1)*	0.48	(2)
Rambo	6.10	(5)	2.44	(2)
Regular	0.09	(1)	0.27	(3)
Expected Revenue	$6.43		$3.19	

* The brackets show the numbers of players.

Note, the expected revenue per round remains constant despite the speed of the dealer. The goal, then, for management is to maximize the total number of rounds that a player goes through. Since rambos drop the most per round, management should strive to get them through as many rounds of blackjack games as possible. As high-limit tables possess most of the rambos, a high-limit table's expected revenue is more than double the expected revenue from a low-limit table. Thus, management should staff these tables with the more proficient dealers.

Neophytes comprise 30 percent of the total dealer population, and experts and intermediates represent 40 percent and 30 percent, respectively. Therefore, of the 36 dealers employed in a single pit, 11 would be neophytes, 11 intermediates, and 14 experts. With a pit having 30 tables (15 high-limit and 15 low-limit), staffing should attempt to fill all high-limit tables with experts (and intermediates, if needed) and all low-limit tables with neophytes:

	High-Limit Tables	Low-Limit Tables	Totals
Neophytes	0	11	11
Intermediates	4	7	11
Experts	14	0	14
Totals	18	18	36

Observations

The data came from observing dealers for several hours. Observations included the following:

- time to complete a shoe (i.e., 208 cards),
- number of deals per shoe,
- time to shuffle,
- time to change money,
- time to rearrange the chip tray,
- time that the dealer was involved in conversation with players, and
- time that the dealer was involved in conversation with pit bosses.

Data from the observations were incorporated into the activities section.

Activity Changes

The government regulates and standardizes dealer actions. Thus, no changes to the "dealing" process were possible. One idea was to mechanize certain aspects of the process (e.g., automating the shuffle). The games manager quickly dashed this idea, saying that players mistrust any kind of machine involvement in a card game. However, two opportunities exist for improving the performance of activities. First, divide the dealers into neophyte, intermediate, and expert. This categorization enables appropriate work assignments and training. Second, categorize players as fun-seekers, rambos, and regulars. These categorizations enable optimal assignment of dealers to players to maximize profits.

Activity Times

Standard times came from a combination of observations, activity changes, and interviews with managers and dealers. Exhibit H shows these standards; the more important standard numbers of deals per hour, by dealer types, are shown below:

	Deals Per Hour	Rounds Per Hour
Neophyte	220	31
Intermediate	278	40
Expert	371	53

These standards apply to seven players at a table. They can be prorated for fewer players.

Activity Drivers

The number of players would be the activity driver. Although there were no historical data, this did not detract from the proposed improvements. The recommended changes apply to all activity levels.

Scheduling

Interviews with several pit bosses revealed that staffing was a totally random process. That is, a dealer's relative experience did not influence table assignment. Any table took any dealer. Thus, an "average dealer" method of staffing existed.

A two-step calculation is needed to estimate the revenue from this method of staffing. First, determine the number of rounds dealt per hour per table:

$$0.3 \text{ [neophyte]} \times 31 \text{ rounds per hour}$$
$$+ \ 0.3 \text{ [intermediate]} \times 40 \text{ rounds per hour}$$
$$+ \ 0.4 \text{ [expert]} \times 53 \text{ rounds per hour}$$
$$= \ 42.5 \text{ rounds per hour}$$

Second, multiply the yields per round by the rounds per hour:

High-Limit Tables	Low-Limit Tables
$6.43 per round	$3.19 per round
× 42.5 rounds per hour	× 42.5 rounds per hour
= $273.28 per hour	= $135.58 per hour

The total revenue for the present staffing method, with 15 high-limit and 15 low-limit tables, is $6,132.90 per hour.

In contrast to the average dealer model, the recommended method would produce more, as demonstrated below. The first step is to calculate the rounds per hour at the two types of tables, with high-yield tables specifically assigned the faster dealers. With that, calculate the yield per table per hour.

EXHIBIT H: TYPICAL ACTIVITY TIME BREAKDOWNS

		Activity	Time Allocation (%)
EXPERT	1	Deal	55.9
	2	Shuffle	16.4
	3	Change Money	5.6
	4	Organize Chip Tray*	0.6
	5	Converse*	1.5
	6	Shift Change	20.0
			100.0
INTERMEDIATE	1	Deal	56.1
	2	Shuffle	15.9
	3	Change Money	5.9
	4	Organize Chip Tray*	1.4
	5	Converse*	0.7
	6	Shift Change	20.0
			100.0
NEOPHYTE	1	Deal	60.2
	2	Shuffle	9.7
	3	Change Money	6.8
	4	Organize Chip Tray*	0.3
	5	Converse*	3.2
	6	Shift Change	20.0
			100.0
STANDARDS	1	Deal	57.0
	2	Shuffle	15.0
	3	Change Money	6.0
	4	Organize Chip Tray*	1.0
	5	Converse*	1.0
	6	Shift Change	20.0
			100.0

* These activities usually occur with dealing or shuffling, and not separately.

High-Limit Tables

0.8 [expert] × 53 rounds per hour = 42.4
0.2 [intermediate] × 40 rounds per hour = 8

Thus, there will be 50.4 rounds per hour (42.4 + 8), and the yield will be $324.07 per table per hour (50.4 × $6.43).

Low-Limit Tables

0.4 [intermediate] × 40 rounds per hour = 16
0.6 [neophyte] × 31 rounds per hour = 18.6

Thus, there will be 34.6 rounds per hour (16 + 18.6), and the yield will be $110.37 per table per hour (34.6 × $3.19).

Total revenue for the recommended method, with the same tables, is $6,516.60 per hour, for a $383.70 improvement or 6.2 percent. The advantage of the recommended assignment of dealer to tables is, therefore, $25.58 per table per hour.

Information System

Games managers should forecast the expected number of customers prior to a shift. This forecast should include a breakdown between the three types of clients, which enable games managers to forecast the tables needed and the high-limit and low-limit breakdown. With that information, they are then able to schedule dealers and forecast the expected revenue for the shift.

The feedback information should consist of actual results by number of clients, number of tables, number of dealers, and total revenue. The actuals — the number of clients and revenue, in particular — should be compared to expectations, and the differences should be analyzed. This results of the analysis should be used to improve forecasts and estimates for future shifts.

Conclusion

This application reveals that there is definite room for improvement with regard to staffing. With the help of management accounting, the casino can analyze its operations and deploy its resources more effectively. The recommended model showed a 6.2 percent improvement in revenues over the existing scheduling method. Note, this model does not look at the potential improvement from setting expectations for dealers as to rounds and revenue per hour.

SECTION II

Management Accounting Cases

Atcom Manufacturing

Atcom is an international firm that specializes in the manufacture of telecommunication equipment. It was the manufacturing subsidiary and major supplier to a provincial telephone utility. With its early success, Atcom started to sell to customers other than its parent. Then, as part of a privatization policy, the provincial government issued 40 percent of Atcom's common shares to the citizens of the province.

Subsequently, Atcom expanded to a national and, more recently, an international (with one plant in the United States) sales and manufacturing organization. Two years ago, under pressure from customers and potential customers, the parent sold all but 10 percent of its shares. That divestment became part of a strategic plan that emphasized an increased level of new product introduction, especially in respect to computer and electronic technologies.

Within the last year, this accelerated introduction of new products has led to problems with the firm's standard cost system. To explain these problems, it is necessary to understand the various controls that are in place at Atcom. Atcom adopted its parent's control system, with few changes. Thus, Atcom updates its long-range (10-year) plan every two years. Quarterly updates supplement the annual budget and monthly reports against the original budget. Plans and budgets emphasize accountability, and they are done at all levels designated as profit, revenue, or cost centres. The MIS department prepares reports on nonfinancial information, e.g., capacity utilization, product quality, customer satisfaction. Sales forecasts are the basis of the budgets, and standards are the basis for production costs.

With this overlay of planning, budgeting, and management information systems, every unit of the organization is subject to standard operating activities, an inheritance from the utility parent. Documented activities specify exactly how employees are to undertake their responsibilities. With each unit an experienced staff (who reports to the president) develops the standards. The detailed operating activities specify the steps that employees must perform, parts, materials, etc. In this way, operating activities provide the basis for evaluating employee performance.

The problem with the standard costs is a result of the rapid rate of new product introduction. The eventually established operating activities are often different and inconsistent with costs committed for new products. Consequently, standard costs may be impossible to meet, or they could be insufficiently demanding. Employees are uncertain about the reasonableness of committed costs, and often there is a lack of motivation to achieve perceived unfair standards.

The president hired you to provide advice on how to resolve the standard cost problem and to get commitment to the budgets and timetable for new products. Within the first few days, you realize that there are two opinions. Among the manufacturing employees, particularly the supervisors, the consensus is that they want to develop detailed activities (i.e., standard operating procedures) before committing to standard costs. They recognize and welcome the expectation that there will be a learning curve and lower unit costs as production volumes increase. However, they insist upon a factual starting point consisting of activities by the accountable employees.

The other consensus comes from the marketing people. They say the standards cannot wait for the detailed activities that determine the standard costs. They admit to the thoroughness and reduced risk from activities-based standard costs. They insist, however, that taking the time to establish the detailed activities will delay the introduction schedule for each new product by between six months and one year, and delay has already caused problems for them. To resolve the conflict they suggest that standard costs should be expected results, from which several different sets of activities could then be selected. Some marketing people are even questioning the need for standard costs. They cite, as evidence in favour of eliminating standard costs, just-in-time inventory systems, the large proportion of purchased components, and the declining share of costs going to direct labour.

Required The president has asked you to implement a solution for introducing new products without delay or lack of control. You are to use the case approach.

Bert the Baker

You are a management accountant with the divisional accounting office of a large grocery retailer, Foodco. Your supervisor has asked you to go to the Richville store to resolve an issue the store manager has with the bakery manager about the fairness of the accounting information used with a bonus system.

In order to remain viable and to grow, Foodco introduced sales and profit targets for retail stores. For an "A-type" store like the Richville store, the weekly sales target is $12 per square foot, or for this 20,000 square-foot store, $12.5 million a year. Operating profits are to be 5 percent of target sales, or $625,000 a year.

Typically, store managers delegate responsibility for sales and operating profits to department managers, i.e., produce, dry goods, bakery, and meats. With this system, the store managers and their department managers receive bonuses equal to about one third of their salaries if the targets are achieved.

Upon arriving at the Richville store, you meet Stella, the store manager, and then Bert, the baker. Bert reiterates his complaint that the bonus system is based on unfair accounting.

I am told that my sales target is $1.75 million a year or about $33,655 a week. I have no problem with sales. I can provide customers with what they want at competitive prices. However, I have a problem with my annual profit target of $150,000, which is 8.5 percent of sales. My complaint has nothing to do with the 8.5 percent profit target being more than the 5 percent for the overall store. A bakery has a better chance of high profits than the other departments.

Let me explain. First, I have little control over my labour costs. The store manager schedules employees who may or may not be necessary for the bakery. Second, the bakery operating statement includes charges that have nothing to do with the bakery. For example, the store manager's total salary is charged to the bakery because it is always profitable. Third, I do not get the chance to approve any of the costs charged to the bakery department. Fourth, I do not receive a copy of the bakery operating statement. Fifth, and most important, there is no opportunity to plan the operating costs in conjunction with the store manager and the other department managers. This would allow costs to be managed more carefully.

Required As the management accountant, you are to use the case approach to identify and analyze the issues and make recommendations for their resolution.

41

Binson's Country Markets

Binson's was established as a fruit and vegetable business vendor in 1929, when Arthur (age 18) and Robert Binson (age 16) began delivering produce from a truck in Toronto. They were joined by their brothers, Jack and Gordon, and their father Fred. In 1939 they moved their business to a store at 1114 St. Clair Avenue in Toronto, which was called Binson's Fruit Market. At that time, all four brothers and their father Fred worked in the store. Ruby, Ethel, Doris, Gwen, Mary and Ruth assisted in the store, making it a true family business. During the war years, Art and Jack stayed home to keep the business going while Bob and Gord served with the army. Following the war, the brothers again delivered their produce in the west end of Toronto, this time in a large bus which was converted into a store on wheels. The name, Binson's, was placed on the front of the bus.

In 1956 Gord and his family purchased the existing property in Newmarket, which is north of Toronto. The original Newmarket store was operational from the May 24th weekend until Thanksgiving each year to sell local fruit and vegetables to travellers. Customers, largely from Toronto, were travelling north each Friday to their cottages and returning on Sunday. In 1967, a grandson, John, was made manager; he immediately kept the store opened 12 months a year, which was possible with the steady customer flow caused by the population growth of Newmarket and surrounding towns and the steady supply of fruit and vegetables from the United States and other spots in the south. Another grandson, Ray, joined the business in 1975, and they started a second store in a nearby community, Aurora. The two grandsons had outstanding success in expanding the product lines and customer base at the two stores. Most important was the brand image of Binson's for fresh, high quality products.

John and Ray died late last year in a car accident. You have just acquired the business from their estates. With the strong brand recognition of Binson's Country Markets, you are planning to expand the number of stores into a chain in Ontario and elsewhere in Canada and North America.

You quickly learn that the two present stores were run effectively and efficiently by John and Ray, who were non-traditional but outstanding managers. John managed the Newmarket store (with about 100 employees) and looked after all ordering and merchandising. Ray managed the Aurora Store (with about 80 employees), as well as all advertisement and promotion. They co-operated fully and worked long hours. They directed all employees in their respective stores with firm but gentle hands. There were no other managers or supervisors, and there were no written procedures or reports. Annually, a local chartered accountant prepared the financial statements for statutory and income tax reasons.

With the help of two long-time employees you have run the two stores for the last three months. One of these employees worked in the Newmarket deli, while the other worked with produce in the Aurora store. Although both were hardworking and dedicated employees, neither of them had had any supervisory experience. Consequently, the employee scheduling was not being done carefully. The employees basically scheduled themselves. The result was that during the busy periods when customers shopped (Thursday and Friday nights and Saturday and Sunday during the day), there were very few employees. Employees made themselves available during week days, when the customers were less prevalent.

You admit that you have not had the time to properly schedule employees to departments or to ensure an adequate level of customer service without excessive costs. In hindsight, there has been excess staffing at times, and inadequate staffing at other times.

As there was only one income statement prepared after the year end (Exhibit 1), you were unclear as to the profitability of each store. Simi-

EXHIBIT 1: NET INCOME STATEMENT, LAST YEAR ($ 000s)

Sales		$31,838
Cost of goods sold		
Opening inventory	4,943	
Purchases	21,603	
Ending inventory	(4,259)	22,287
General and administrative expenses		
Employee salaries, wages, benefits	1,552	
Rent	1,184	
Amortization (non vehicle)	543	
Utilities	458	
Materials and supplies	720	
Vehicle expenses	722	
Advertisement and promotion	1,865	
Other expenses	167	7,211
Net income before income taxes		$ 2,340

EXHIBIT 2: SALES BREAKDOWN BY STORE, LAST YEAR ($ 000s)

Department	Newmarket	Aurora
Bakery, fresh breads	$ 3,766	$ 2,866
Bulk foods	643	569
Dairy	571	450
Deli meats and cheeses	4,940	3,276
Deliver, e-mail sales	747	627
Flowers	465	324
Frozen foods	737	657
Groceries	1,849	701
Meat, poultry, fish	2,495	2,569
Olive bar, salad bar	948	877
Prepared foods	518	484
Produce (fruit and vegetables)	449	311
Total	$18,128	$13,711

larly, you were unclear of the profitability of each department in each store, other than the sales by department, which are captured by the cash registers (Exhibit 2).

You realize that a professional general manager will need to be hired for each store. These two managers will report directly to you along with a project team for expanding the number of stores, a controller, and a director of advertisement and promotion. From an examination of the sales by department for each store, you estimate that six supervisors might be needed at each store. Each supervisor will need to be responsible for one or more sales departments.

In considering the assignment of departments to supervisors, the following appears to be a preliminary arrangement:

- Bakery, fresh breads
- Bulk foods, groceries
- Dairy, frozen foods
- Deli meats, cheese, olive bar, salad bar, prepared foods, delivery, e-mail sales
- Meat, poultry, fish
- Produce (fruit and vegetables), flowers

You recognize that for the future well-being of the stores, nonfinancial measures are necessary. However, as a first step you want to establish a management accounting system that will ensure profitability of departments and stores with return on sales and return on investment. You want to use the new system for the two existing stores as well all new stores.

You have been considering the installation of new loading docks at the Newmarket and the Aurora stores. The new dock will speed up unloading and thereby get the goods on the shelves more quickly. The new equipment will cost $300,000, and it will have a life of 10 years with a salvage value of $50,000. The vendor will finance 90 percent of the value at six percent per year. As more goods will be on the shelves sooner and longer, you expect sales to increase by $100,000 per year. The main advantage will be that the new equipment will save $50,000 annually in labour costs. The cost of capital is eight percent, and the tax shield equals

$$\text{Tax Shield Rate} = \frac{T \times C}{C + R} \times \frac{2 + R}{2(1 + R)}$$

where

T = the income tax rate, 30 percent
C = the CCA rate, 30 percent
R = the cost of capital or required rate of return, eight percent.

Required Use the case approach to specify the management accounting requirements and to assess the proposal for new loading docks.

Brights Lodging and Travel

Some owners of hotel properties have been establishing new medium-priced, good quality hotels in dilapidated downtown locations. The new properties are either new buildings built on vacant land or major renovations to existing buildings, previously used for other purposes. There are two reasons for placing new hotels into seedy downtown areas where the neighbours might include ramshackle rows of shops, nightclubs with bullet-proof glass, and homeless people. First, there is the strategy of developing up-and-coming locations in major U.S. cities, and thereby taking advantage of the expected return of people to inner cities. These properties are a bet on urban renewals and increased property values. Second, these downtown hotels provide convenient accommodations for busy business travellers who want good quality without paying for unnecessary opulence. They are also a wager on a change in business practices from opulence to basic quality saving travellers money and increasing the returns to hotels.

There is a simple but consistent format for each hotel chain participating in these urban renewals. For one major chain the rooms surround a central pool, there is plenty of parking for rental cars, all rooms have functional desks and data ports for laptops, and the modest lobbies have breakfast buffets. Their uniformity makes these urban renewals easy to spot, and thereby reduces the need for advertisement.

A new building on vacant land does not pose any significant problems. Renovating existing alternative use buildings can have problems, and these renovations may be 20 to 30 percent more expensive than comparable new buildings. Renovations may be further complicated. Antiquated plumbing and electrical systems often are more expensive to rebuild than to replace with new systems. Older buildings have layouts that pose challenges. One renovation example is where two king-size beds fit in room 801 but not into 701. The problem is that the building's walls are inches thicker at the base,

making the lower-floor rooms smaller. Nevertheless, renovations are often required to meet specific municipal regulations.

During the past year, Brights Lodging and Travel Corporation (BLT) has managed 26 of these urban renewal hotels, and it has signed an agreement to manage another six for another hotel chain starting next year. It should be noted that there are often two players in the delivery of hotel services. First, there are the owners of the hotel buildings, such as those developing no-frills urban renewals. Second, there are the management companies, such as BLT, that manage the hotels. The latter hire all employees, buy all supplies and food, and maintain all equipment and facilities. These management firms work on the basis of a share of the top-line revenue or a share in the profits.

As the management accountant at BLT you have been asked by the board of directors and the CEO (who is a member of the board and a major shareholder of BLT) to develop a balanced scorecard. She recently attended a hotel management conference where there was a session on the benefits from using the balanced scorecard. To advise you, the CEO has formed a committee consisting of herself, the controller, two owner representatives, and three general managers from successful BLT-managed hotels.

The committee established a series of meetings to exchange information for guiding you with the balanced scorecard. In the end, they provided you with advice on all four perspectives of the balanced scorecard.

Financial Perspective

The committee noted that financial measures have been the basis for gauging the effectiveness of hotel management, despite other factors such as customer satisfaction and employee (associate) turnover having a direct effect on financial performance. BLT uses ACCPAC to produce operating statements for each hotel and chain, with the format shown in Exhibit 1. The hotel example in the exhibit has 297 rooms for rent 365 days a year, and an annual occupancy rate of 80 percent for the most recent year. (Occupancy is the number of rooms occupied divided by the total rooms available.) This occupancy level is above average but not exceptional. Ninety percent of the revenues come from room rentals. There are four classes of expenses: cost of goods sold, payroll, controllable, and uncontrollable.

BLT monitors performances at the property (i.e., hotel) and corporate (all properties managed for a chain) levels to ensure the owners' long-term objectives are being met. Presently, BLT manages a portfolio of 26 hotels with annual sales of $278 million. This sales volume represents substantial growth during the last decade when the company started with twelve hotels and $63 million in annual revenues. BLT's board of directors, consisting of all shareholders of BLT, wants sales to grow at the rate of 15 percent per year for the next decade with hotel profitability maintained at the current levels. The board also wants BLT-managed hotels to outperform competitors. Although BLT-managed hotels are doing well, they are not meeting the expectation of the board:

- they are *not* in the top 20 percent in guest scores and profitability;
- the turnover rate of hourly employees is *not* less than 60 percent annually;
- the turnover rate of managers is *not* less than 20 percent annually;
- budgets are *not* always achieved; and
- owners' unlevered returns on investment are *not* always equal to or greater than 15 percent.

More specifically, the BLT committee agreed on two financial measures for the balanced scorecard. The first indicator was a yield index that gauges a property's revenue per available room (RevPAR) relative to competitive hotels as well as to year-over-year improvement. The inherent objective is to achieve both higher RevPAR levels and faster RevPAR growth rates than those of competitors. The second indicator is an index of operating performance relative to a flexible budget. Rather than focusing on property-profit achievement relative to budget, the committee designed this index, which is part of the operating statement in Exhibit 1, to consider only expenses that are controllable by hotel general managers and, simultaneously, adjust expected performance to account for variances in business volume (occupancy). The committee called this a flow-through model, and with it they expected the following:

EXHIBIT 1: OPERATING STATEMENT

	Latest Year
Rooms available	108,405
Rooms occupied	86,714
Average rate	82.79
Revenue	
Rooms	$7,179,052
Food	306,198
Beverage	51,203
Telephone	289,890
Other	138,468
Total	7,964,811
Cost of goods sold	
Telephone	42,257
Telephone equipment	22,893
Other	311,001
Total cost of goods	376,151
Payroll	
Housekeeping	466,472
Laundry	53,987
Front desk	122,550
Administration	86,123
Sales	27,024
Maintenance	82,286
Management (salary)	279,335
Employee relations	25,670
Other	121,455
Total payroll	1,264,902
Controllable expenses	
Linen and laundry	46,826
Guest supplies	70,983
Cleaning expense	44,867
Rooms, other	92,022
Postage	9,750
Office supplies	20,748
Administration telephone	19,032
Travel	15,459
Cashier (overage) or shortage	364
Bad debt expense	7,965
Administration, other	35,274
Advertising	21,840
Maintenance supplies	9,165
Maintenance trash	29,303
Maintenance	99,489
Utilities	275,360
House charges, other	49,686
Total controllable expenses	848,133
Total operating expenses	2,489,186
Contribution to profits	5,475,625
Uncontrollable expenses	1,590,392
House profit	$3,885,233

- meet budget targets,
- demonstrate superior financial management of hotels,
- outperform competitors in profitability and expense-control,
- achieve internal consistency in property operations, and
- deliver high investment returns to owners.

The committee was particularly pleased with the flow-through model's ability to re-forecast controllable costs using a fixed and variable cost model to adjust performance expectations to reflect actual room rentals. Line items that vary with respect to occupancy are re-forecasted every period that actual occupancy differs from budgeted occupancy. The result is a line item entitled, "Contribution to house profit from controllable items." This line item incorporates expenditures over which the general manager has considerable control, e.g., payroll, utilities, maintenance, office supplies. However, it does not include items over which the general manager has little or no control, e.g., franchise fees, health and welfare insurance, travel-agent commissions. The advantage of excluding uncontrollable items is that general managers can be held to a higher level of accountability for items that they control without facing the frustration of unanticipated changes to uncontrollable items.

An additional benefit of the flow-through model as a management tool is that it allows owners to focus on management and cost control issues that might otherwise be buried within the financial operating statement. Those factors are exposed in the variance calculations for each line item that is under management control.

The committee recognized that measuring operating performance strictly on financial measures is inconsistent with the long-term investment horizon and with BLT's corporate objectives. Furthermore, they repeatedly noted that financial measures are lagging indicators rather than leading indicators and cannot be used to predict future performance. BLT needs, according to the committee, measures that track financial results while simultaneously monitoring progress in building the capability and acquiring the intangible assets needed for future growth. The committee agreed that the balanced scorecard must have the following characteristics:

- not limited to financial performance;
- nonfinancial performance measures dealing with factors important for long-term growth and value creation;
- inclusion of factors that lead to growth, profitability, and physical maintenance;
- simple to monitor; and

- easy for general managers to understand and accept.

Customer Perspective
The committee reviewed the following potential guest-related indicators: customer satisfaction, customer retention, new-customer acquisition, market segmentation, market share, customer profitability, responsiveness, associate knowledge and service levels, and mystery-guest assessments.

Internal research found that guest scores correlate with investment returns, thus substantiating the value to owners of high guest-satisfaction levels. Properties that scored in the top 20 percent of guest-satisfaction scores provided investment returns averaging 17.4 percent in the most recent year. Properties that scored in the top 40 percent of the guest-satisfaction scores still managed a 15.2 percent, while properties below median levels provided only a 12.7 percent return.

Internal Business Processes
The committee evaluated a number of internal business process measures that might bear on the objectives of both management and owners, including the following: associate-productivity rates, service errors and failure rates, maintenance of physical assets, capital-expenditure efficiency, accounting and internal-control practices, and time required to complete key processes and tasks, e.g., check-in, maintenance, breakfast seating and serving.

BLT predominantly manages national franchise affiliations; thus, general managers have only minimal control over the matters relating to marketing and brand recognition. Furthermore, a number of the indicators dealing with efficiency and productivity rates are indirectly reflected in the financial flow-through model. The committee developed a comprehensive hotel audit program to check and verify that general managers comply with the internal business process expectations or standards. These criteria are shown in Exhibit 2. Each audit is to be conducted by a manager of internal audit against a detailed check list of items. If there is compliance to all items, the hotel (i.e., its general manager) receives a perfect control of 100 points. Hotels receiving less than 90 points are expected to have serious operating shortcomings. Only with more than 97.5 points will general managers be excused from remedial actions.

Learning and Growth
The committee considered the following possible measures to gauge the learning and growth:

- personal growth of associates (employees);

EXHIBIT 2: OUTLINE OF BLT CONSOLIDATED PROCESS AUDIT

Human-resources best practices

1. Personnel files are properly maintained, e.g., reviews, discipline, tax forms
2. Associates adhere to training schedules
3. Uniforms are worn per policy
4. Hotel complies with provincial and federal human resources regulations

Hotel-improvement best practices

1. Associates are aware of mission statement, critical success factors
2. Guest rooms and public areas are properly cleaned and inspected
3. Defects and guest complaints are properly recorded and resolved
4. Sales and marketing goals are posted and results tracked properly
5. Hotel adheres to accounting and internal-control processes

Maintenance best practices

1. Guest rooms and public areas are refreshed with quarterly preventive maintenance
2. Major equipment items are maintained according to schedule
3. Inspections are kept current, e.g., fire, elevator, health
4. Pool readings are conducted and logged correctly
5. Capital-expenditure file is maintained correctly

- internal promotion levels;
- associate satisfaction;
- associate retention;
- associate empowerment;
- strategic skills of associates, managers, and the organization; training levels and cycle times;
- cross-training levels of associates and line manager;
- information technology use;
- access to strategic information;
- new initiatives explored or implemented; and
- community participation and knowledge exhibited by general managers.

With a median associate turnover rate of 88.3 percent, BLT experienced many personnel issues common to the hospitality industry. That level of turnover meant the company was constantly replacing workers, spending time and energy on training, and experiencing reduced guest-satisfaction levels because of mistakes made by inexperienced associates. Thus, associate (employee) retention presented the greatest opportunity for improvement within the organization. Furthermore, the committee determined that many of the other measures, although valid, would be ineffective in the absence of a stable base of long-term associates. A supplemental analysis showed that hotels with associate turnover below 100 percent (which is still substantial) enjoyed generally higher profit and RevPAR growth than those with turnover levels exceeding 100 percent. Given the negative impact of associate turnover, the committee recommended that the balanced scorecard emphasize the reduction in turnover levels.

Required As the management accountant and a member of the balanced scorecard committee, use the case approach to complete the balanced scorecard for BLT.

CCP Publishers

You have been hired by Chris Paraskevopoulos, who is an economics professor emeritus at your university. Chris is a familiar figure on campus particularly as he has a striking resemblance to the actor Walter Mathis. After retiring from teaching, Chris started an academic publishing business, which publishes university textbooks and trade books, the latter being academic books written by university professors for academic and professional audiences.

CCP Publishers is located on the 10th floor of a building in the northern part of the city. It also leases 500 square metres in the basement of the building for its warehouse operations. Chris is the chief editor as well as the CEO. There are four editors in addition to Chris, three editorial assistants, four marketing representatives, a business manager (yourself), and a warehouse supervisor. Chris and the four editors are all equal partners. The marketing representatives are responsible for selling CCP books to university and commercial bookstores.

The business model has changed little since CCP was established three years ago. Authors either contact an editor or the editor contacts the author. In either situation, when there is an agreement between the author (or authors) and an editor that the book will be economically viable, a contract is signed that specifies the general content of the book, a publication schedule, and responsibilities for both CCP and the author or authors. An editor from CCP works with each author (or author group) in the development of a book. Currently, 35 books are in various stages of production. CCP has 42 books in print and available for sale. Most activities are contracted out, including copyediting, layout, index development, art work, photography, and printing. After printing, books are shipped directly to university and commercial bookstores.

The income statement for the latest fiscal year is shown below:

Sales	$975,000
Cost of books sold	(210,000)
Salaries and wages	(540,000)
Rental	(87,000)
Shipping	(62,000)
Miscellaneous	(52,000)
Operating income	$24,000

Chris has some concerns about the profitability of CCP. He believes that CCP should be more profitable. He would like to control the development costs for book. He would also like to know the profitability of each book and how that profitability compares with expectations of the editor when the contract is signed. Consequently, you were hired as the business manager.

Required As the business manager, use the case approach to address the CEO's profitability concerns.

Clearwater Small Appliances

Clearwater manufactures a wide range of small household appliances such as coffee makers, can openers, microwave and toaster ovens, irons and ironing boards. In 50 years of existence, it has prospered and established a well-respected brand name. Business has been good — at least up to now. Recent changes in methods of retailing require Clearwater to alter significantly its way of doing business. Traditionally, Clearwater has supplied retailers such as department stores, hardware stores, and discount stores. They now are suffering declining sales because giant category retailers like Home Depot, Canadian Tire, Wal-Mart, and Zellers dominate the market. These "power retailers" use sophisticated information and inventory management. Their finely tuned selections and competitive pricing crowd out weaker retailers. The forecast is that category retailers will continue gaining market share.

So powerful have category retailers become that they tell even the largest and most powerful manufacturers what goods to make, in what colours and sizes, and how much to ship and when. In fact, they dictate practically all terms of business with their suppliers. Some category retailers even charge the manufacturers for shipment errors. They constantly squeeze costs; for example, some have operating and selling expenses as low as 15 percent of sales, compared to 28 percent for traditional department stores. The difference is even greater than these 13 percentage points, as the sales prices are about 5 percent lower for the category retailers than for department stores.

In order to survive, Clearwater must supply category stores; to be a supplier, Clearwater must tailor its products to please individual category retailers and meet high standards for on time, defect-free merchandise. However, Clearwater wants to preserve its brand name "Clearwater" instead of merely manufacturing store brands. Supplying category retailers is, for Clearwater, only a coping strategy. It recognizes that it needs to supply the category retailers, but it also recognizes that to survive, Clearwater must have a separate and strong identity.

The management team developed a new strategy. In formulating it, they sought substantial input from all parts of Clearwater. As well, buyers and executives from three of the largest category retailers provided insights about what changes would be required to meet their needs. The result is the following internal statement endorsed by the board of directors.

TACTICS FOR COPING WITH CATEGORY RETAILERS

- **Protect our brands.** If customers ask for our products by name, the category retailers are more likely to stock our products. Consequently, we must advertise, and not merely depend on the category retailers for exposure.

- **Customize.** Meet customer requirements — whether category retailer or customer.

- **Innovate constantly.** Non-distinguishable products are vulnerable because category retailers can readily replace suppliers or contract for the manufacture of their own brands.

- **Organize around the category retailer.** The organization will reorganize into multi-disciplinary teams, each of which will serve the largest category retailers.

- **Invest in technology.** The category retailers demand the latest information technology to ensure that the right products arrive on the shelves at the right time.

- **Cut the fat.** If we do not constantly reduce our costs and pass the savings on to the category retailers, they will find manufacturers that can and do.

You, as the vice-president controller, with the management team, have been fully involved in formulating the strategy by which to become a profitable supplier to category retailers. You are now to develop an information system for planning (i.e., budgeting one to three years into the future) and monitoring the strategy. This information is to be incorporated into the monthly cost of quality report, which operation you are also to review and make any necessary changes to improve its usefulness.

COST OF QUALITY REPORT

Prevention

Quality engineering
Receiving inspection
Quality training

Appraisal

Product inspection

Internal Failures

Scrap
Rework

External Failures

Net cost of returned products

The cost of quality report is compiled monthly by the production vice-president and one of the production scheduling engineers, using estimates based on their experience. Separate tracking and budgeting do not occur for these costs. The production vice-president is responsible for quality, but many of her subordinates are in better positions for ensuring it.

Required Undertake your project using the case approach and report your findings to the management committee.

CASE 7

Coffee Maker Supreme

Coffee Maker Supreme (CMS) has been in the business of manufacturing coffee makers for three generations. During the first and second generations the growth in demand was modestly positive, and customers seemed to have been more content with product range and quality. During the time of the present generation of owners, the demand for coffee machines grew at a much higher rate. That demand does not appear to be declining in the foreseeable future. Moreover, customers have become increasingly demanding of specialized and high-quality coffee makers.

CMS is a privately owned manufacturer and distributor of machines to make coffee. Sales are more than $200 million per year. Customers — from all parts of world — are restaurants, cafes, and cafeterias. Sales are made by commissioned sales representatives supported by a website to process orders and to provide after-sales service. CMS started in the Canadian market, but expanded into the United States a decade before the free-trade agreement. Nicole Roberto joined the business after completing her CMA. Two years earlier, she had completed her undergraduate degree in business. She encouraged her father to purchase coffee machine manufacturers in France and Italy in order to expand into the European market. She then spent a decade in Europe developing the business. Her heritage language — Italian — and her French immersion studies from grades 1 to 12 assisted her in successfully developing the European business.

In 1997, the sales representatives from around the world were provided with Web-based sales support for transacting sales and for the customers to obtain post-sales service and support. This system proved highly successful, allowing CMS to further expand into Europe and into the Japanese and Mexican markets. The global reach with plants in Canada, the United States, France and Italy meant that there was a rather haphazard product line. The four plants produced 27 products, of which 10 were literally duplicates of another 10, resulting in only 17 truly different products. In 2000, the product line was rationalized, allowing two of the plants to be closed and for the product line to be increased by 13 new coffee makers that were different from existing products. Of the current 30 different coffee makers, 16 are manufactured in one plant and 14 are manufactured in the other. In effect, the new products expanded both ends of the product line, i.e., both larger-capacity and small special-purpose coffee makers. Moreover, features were added to make all coffee makers more versatile. In effect, each of the 30 products experienced product design and manufacturing process changes.

Global sourcing was introduced at the same time to ensure procurement of the most appropriate and cost-effective materials and components. Along with global sourcing, the decades-old practice of 100 percent inspection was replaced with a more modern system of random checks. This allowed for most of the inspectors to be reassigned. Suppliers were responsible for quality of all materials and components, and manufacturing workers were responsible for quality control in the manufacturing process. Each worker knew the operating specifications, and if a unit received at his or her station was not up to standard, the manufacturing process could be stopped for the necessary corrections.

The financial results of the first full year of operations with the product line and related changes are shown in Exhibit 1. These results were what president Nicole Roberto showed you as you started your first day as the controller. Nicole had been brought back to Canada three months earlier when the previous president had been obliged to retire for health reasons.

The first task assigned to you by Nicole was to determine why, when sales targets were met, operating income was substantially lower than budget. You first reviewed the variance. The sales variance at one percent was trivial. After talking to the manufacturing vice-president, who was in charge of both plants, you concluded that the mate-

EXHIBIT 1: OPERATING STATEMENT, YEAR T (MILLIONS OF DOLLARS)

	Budget	Actual	Variance
Sales	$216.0	$218.3	$ 2.3
Cost of Goods Sold			
Variable costs:			
Materials	62.7	64.8	(2.1)
Manufacturing labour	10.6	11.4	(0.8)
Manufacturing overhead	23.7	25.1	(1.4)
Selling	8.6	8.7	(0.1)
	105.6	110.0	(4.4)
Contribution Margin	110.4	108.3	(2.1)
Fixed Expenses			
Manufacturing overhead	49.4	66.1	(16.7)
Selling	10.7	10.6	0.1
Administration	18.6	18.7	(0.1)
	78.7	95.4	(16.7)
Operating Income	$ 31.7	$ 12.9	$(18.8)

EXHIBIT 2: COST OF QUALITY REPORT (MILLIONS OF DOLLARS)

	Year T	T–1	T–2	T–3	T–4	T–5
Prevention costs	$ 1.2	$3.1	$3.2	$3.0	$2.8	$2.6
Appraisal costs	0.1	1.3	1.4	1.2	1.0	1.0
Internal failure costs	2.1	1.1	1.0	0.7	0.8	0.8
External failure costs	6.7	0.6	0.2	0.6	0.3	0.4
Total quality costs	$10.1	6.1	5.8	5.5	4.9	4.8

EXHIBIT 3: CUSTOMER SATISFACTION SURVEY
(DECEMBER SURVEYS, % SCORE ON A 0% TO 100% SCALE)

	Year T	T–1	T–2	T–3	T–4	T–5
Product quality	61.5	85.5	84.7	85.9	86.1	85.3
Durability	58.3	93.3	92.7	92.2	92.7	93.6
Good value	48.6	75.1	77.5	76.6	78.1	76.4
Features	88.6	53.8	56.3	55.8	54.7	53.1

rial variance is largely attributed to some yield problems with some materials and components and that these yield problems created the unfavourable variances for direct labour and variable manufacturing overhead. A bigger problem was the fixed manufacturing overhead. The manufacturing vice-president explained this variance to be the result of charging to fixed manufacturing overhead, the rework required in getting the plants accustomed to manufacturing the new and newly designed products. Warranty work was also charged to fixed manufacturing overhead, whether an actual or estimated charge. You also asked for and received the cost of quality report (Exhibit 2) and the customer satisfaction survey results (Exhibit 3).

Required As the controller, carry out your assignment using the case approach.

Consolidated Pump

Your firm, Consolidated Pump, is a major manufacturer and distributor of industrial pumps. Due to technological advances in pump design and manufacturing, sales and profits have grown substantially. Other firms, observing this growth, have entered or expanded their presence in the pump market, and consequently competition has intensified. See Exhibits 1 and 2 for the impact of recent competition on financial performance.

The technological advances have been applicable to a wide range of pumps, and Consolidated Pump has purchased several previously autonomous pump manufacturers that produced related products. Consolidated Pump then improved the technology of its pumps and its manufacturing

processes. As a result, Consolidated Pump now produces 87 different products. The number of inventoried parts for making pumps has grown more rapidly than has the number of assembled pumps. Because of the large number of different parts, the purchasing department costs have grown at a particularly rapid rate. This has been a concern, and the business analyst studied these costs. Exhibit 3 shows this analysis.

The standard price equals total cost plus a markup of 80 percent. Product costs equal direct materials, direct labour, and overhead allocated on direct labour hours. In the past, this pricing practice has been satisfactory. Due to near total automation of production, direct labour is now only

---

EXHIBIT 1:   CONSOLIDATED PUMP, SUMMARY OF FINANCIAL STATEMENTS
(IN MILLIONS OF DOLLARS)

	Year T	T–1	T–2	T–3
Sales	$112	$95	$81	$69
Less:				
Variable manufacturing cost of goods sold	15	18	18	22
Variable marketing and administrative costs	8	7	6	4
Total variable costs	23	25	24	26
Contribution margin	89	70	57	43
Deduct:				
Fixed manufacturing costs	50	34	27	18
Fixed marketing and administrative costs	27	24	20	16
Total fixed costs	77	58	47	34
Operating income	12	12	10	9
Net income after taxes	$ 7	$ 7	$ 6	$ 5
Inventories	29	23	19	10
Total assets	50	48	43	39
Long-term bonds	17	19	23	21
Owners' equity	24	19	12	9

EXHIBIT 2: CONSOLIDATED PUMP'S COMPARATIVE PERFORMANCE DATA
(AS A PERCENTAGE OF INDUSTRY TOTAL)

	Sales	Net Income	Total Assets	Owners' Equity
T–11	4.7	5.1	4.5	5.2
T–10	4.9	5.3	4.6	5.5
T–9	4.7	5.4	4.7	5.4
T–8	4.8	5.9	4.5	5.9
T–7	4.9	6.0	5.0	5.8
T–6	5.0	6.4	5.1	6.4
T–5	6.0	7.2	6.2	7.0
T–4	6.4	7.1	6.2	7.4
T–3	7.0	8.5	6.8	7.7
T–2	7.2	12.4	7.7	9.5
T–1	8.6	13.1	7.9	10.2
Year T	9.5	11.4	7.9	10.3

EXHIBIT 3: ANALYSIS OF CONSOLIDATED PUMP'S PURCHASING DEPARTMENT

Senior management has been concerned that costs have increased at an alarming rate in the purchasing department, although the director of purchasing regularly overworks her purchasing agents. The analysis sought to identify the causes of the growth in purchasing department costs and then understand how to control those factors. As a first step, the analyst asked purchasing people what were the reasons for their activities. Although 11 cost drivers were initially identified, after analysis, the director reasoned that three cost drivers were significant: sales, number of different pumps, and number of different parts.

Multiple regression was initially used on the 12 years of data, but multi-collinearity was greater than 0.8. Below are the results from simple regression for three cost drivers (independent variables) and purchasing department total costs (the dependent variable).

Variable	Coefficient*	Standard Error*
Regression Number 1		
Constant	5,702.1	2,741.3
Independent variable 1:		
Sales in dollars ($r^2 = 0.46$)	1.9	1.2
Regression Number 2		
Constant	2,491.7	1,021.6
Independent variable 1:		
Number of different pumps ($r^2 = 0.32$)	61.4	70.3
Regression Number 3		
Constant	40.4	25.8
Independent variable 1:		
Number of different parts ($r^2 = 0.79$)	5.9	1.6

* Elimination of some zeros for the coefficients and standard errors, did not distort the relationships between respective coefficient and standard error.

9 percent of manufacturing costs. Materials are about 10 percent. The remaining 81 percent comes from manufacturing overhead. Senior management has become suspicious of the allocation of over-head based on direct labour; a detailed study of activities found that time in production was a more valid indicator of the manufacturing overhead consumed by a product than direct labour hours. For

---

EXHIBIT 4: ALLOCATION OF CONSOLIDATED PUMP'S COSTS, PRODUCT PRICING

The 87 pumps made by Consolidated Pump can be aggregated into five classes. The cost of an individual pump is a variation of its class, reflecting more or fewer materials and processing time. The idea of a class of pump simplifies production and marketing.

	Class				
	A	**B**	**C**	**D**	**E**
Standard Unit Costs					
Direct Labour	$ 4.22	$ 6.17	$ 7.87	$ 10.48	$ 14.69
Materials	3.40	5.10	6.07	7.92	9.74
Overhead*	31.68	42.24	50.69	71.81	107.71
	$39.30	$53.51	$ 64.63	$ 90.21	$132.14
Consolidated's Standard Price	$70.74	$96.32	$116.33	$162.38	$237.85
Competitors Price	$69.00	$93.00	$114.00	$170.00	$240.00
Units Sold	51,100	52,400	57,400	411,400	127,400
Direct labour hours, actual	1.5	2.0	2.4	3.4	5.1
Time in (hours) production, actual	5.2	7.1	15.0	18.2	26.5

* Manufacturing overhead is allocated to products with the following formula:

$$\frac{\text{Budgeted Overhead in dollars}}{\text{Budgeted Direct Labour in hours}} \times \text{actual direct labour hours}$$

---

this alternative approach to assigning manufacturing overhead, you have gathered the preliminary data contained in Exhibit 4. It is unclear whether there is any value in changing the allocation base.

Parts inventories have been increasing in recent years to where now they are out of control. The annual budget makes provision for a parts inventory based on last year, with adjustments for changes to the product line to be assembled. This approach to inventory planning has led to excesses for some parts and shortages for others. However, the nature of the pump business is that pumps manufactured and shipped represent firm orders. For most pumps, demand is highly predictable, and parts are readily available within one to two days. However, the higher-priced pumps are more difficult to forecast.

Required The controller asked you, a management accountant, to use the case approach to (1) identify the reasons for profit problems through quantitative and qualitative analysis, and (2) recommend solutions.

Construction Equipment Manufacturing Limited

Construction Equipment Manufacturing Limited (CEML) is Canada's largest manufacturer of excavating (digging) equipment. It produces five major product lines through 13 manufacturing divisions and sells these products with one sales division. All manufacturing divisions buy and sell extensively among one another. The sales division is a profit centre.

CEML was established in Saskatchewan in the 1920s to build equipment to extract potash (a fertilizer) from underground mines. After 1950 the company expanded into the manufacturing of other mining equipment, especially for coal mining, but also for all other types of mining. In the late 1970s, CEML expanded into making particularly specialized excavation equipment for the oil sands open-pit mining industry of Alberta. Through the acquisitions of other excavation equipment manufacturers, CEML had, by 1990, become the largest manufacturer and seller of excavation equipment in North America.

CEML initiated in 1995 co-branding and supply agreements with several key suppliers, including a leading European manufacturer of excavation equipment. Then, in 1998, CEML obtained a co-branding supply agreement with a Japanese firm to offer excavator solutions to customers in Asian markets. Presently, Saskatchewan-based CEML is the largest manufacturer and distributor of specialized excavation equipment in the world.

Transfer prices among the manufacturing divisions have been set at standard variable cost plus a 40 percent markup to cover other costs and profit. This transfer price system has been satisfactory for decades. However, recently two changes have occurred to make this transfer price unsatisfactory. First, CEML changed its responsibility accounting system. Now all manufacturing divisions are investment centres rather than cost centres, and the general managers of manufacturing divisions obtain about 30 percent of their take-home income from incentives tied to return on investment (ROI) of their division. Second, outsourcing

of parts is now possible with the overall expansion of the excavation equipment market. As the market became larger, more suppliers came to serve the market; and, increasingly, excavation equipment manufacturers pursued opportunities to outsource, even if this meant purchasing parts from their competitors. This trend is expected to continue.

You are a business analyst in the corporate office of CEML. The chief financial officer has asked you to investigate the transfer price policy and make recommendations, especially regarding the existing transfer pricing arrangement between the Winnipeg division and the Chicago division. The transfer of concern is a motor unit that the Winnipeg division assembles and uses in its own products; plus, it sells these motor units to the Chicago division. (See financial statements for the two manufacturing divisions shown in Exhibits 1 and 2.)

The agreement between the two divisions has been in place for two decades, and from all indications there have been minimal problems. The Winnipeg division has always wanted the transfer pricing to be done on the basis of actual cost rather than standard. In contrast, the Chicago has argued for standard costs for the transfer price. For the current year this transfer equals $75 million in revenue for the Winnipeg division and $75 million in variable manufacturing costs for the Chicago division. This transfer was done at standard variable costs plus 40 percent.

The Chicago division has been approached by a highly reputable manufacturer of engines with an offer of equal quality engine units at a price of $60 million. The general manager of the Chicago division wants to accept the $60 million external offer as it will increase the division's ROI. The Winnipeg general manager is opposed to losing the $75 million sales to the Chicago division. He claims that it would be difficult to replace the lost sales, which would be detrimental to the entire company. Moreover, he says, it would not be fair to set the transfer price at the lower $60 million as

```
                    EXHIBIT 1

                 Winnipeg Division
                 Operating Budget
          For the Year Ending December 31
                   ($ millions)

Revenue:
Outside sales                          $260
Internal sales                          100
                                        360
Variable costs:
Manufacturing                           120
Administration                           40
                                        160
Fixed expenses:
Manufacturing                            80
Administration                           30
Research and development                 40
                                        150

Operating income                      $ 50

Working capital                       $ 50
Net fixed assets                        150
Investment                            $200

ROI (50/200)                           0.25
```

```
                    EXHIBIT 2

                 Chicago Division
                 Operating Budget
          For the Year Ending December 31
                   ($ millions)

Revenue:
Outside sales                          $400
Internal sales                           50
                                        450
Variable costs:
Manufacturing                           170
Administration                           30
                                        200
Fixed expenses:
Manufacturing                           100
Administration                           40
Research and development                 40
                                        180

Operating income                      $ 70

Working capital                       $ 50
Net fixed assets                        175
Investment                            $225

ROI (70/225)                           0.31
```

the Chicago division's higher ROI means that its general manager already has a substantially larger bonus. The Winnipeg general manager said he works about 100 hours per week, and a reduction in his bonus would be an insult.

The two general managers have not been able to reach an agreement. Starting next year the Chicago general manager plans to terminate the transfer agreement with the Winnipeg division and accept the external offer.

In undertaking your assignment, you investigate the offer provided to the Chicago division by the manufacturer of engine units. The vendor, Precision Engines Inc., specializes in engine units for the automotive and truck industries. Currently, those industries are in recessions, and Precision Engines has excess capacity. To supply the order to the Chicago, you estimate that Precision Engines would have had to incur set-up costs to produce a new engine from their production facilities. After covering these set-up costs plus variable costs, you estimate that, with the quoted price, there would not be much left for fixed costs and profits.

The Chicago division has been considering the installation of a new production scheduling system. The chief financial officer also asked you to access its viability. The new system will speed up shipments and, thereby, get the goods to the customers more quickly. The new equipment will cost $600,000, and it will have a life of 10 years with a salvage value of $100,000. The vendor will finance 80 percent of the value at six percent per year. As more goods will be shipped sooner, the division expects sales to increase by $200,000 per year. The main advantage will be that the new equipment will save $100,000 annually in labour costs. The cost of capital is eight percent, and the tax shield equals

$$\text{Tax Shield Rate} = \frac{T \times C}{C + R} \times \frac{2 + R}{2(1 + R)}$$

where
T = the income tax rate, 30 percent
C = the CCA rate, 30 percent
R = the cost of capital or required rate of return, eight percent.

Required Use the case approach to address the tasks assigned to you by the chief financial officer.

Container Plastics Company

Ron Forlani has just gone public and expanded his container business. As a creative and skilled engineer, Ron develops technologically advanced machinery and moulds, which provide Container Plastics with a competitive advantage. Above-average profits come from the technological advantages, but only temporarily, as competitor imitation takes between six months and one year.

Ron has two tactics for addressing this technology copying. First, he plans and works towards continuously introducing technological improvements in processes and products. For example, there is an ongoing goal for production costs to decrease eight percent a year. Second, Container Plastics stresses new products. For example, there is a policy that 25 percent of the sales each year must come from products introduced in the past five years.

Container Plastics is in the plastic products industry, specifically in the rigid packaging sector. Its products include pop bottles, cosmetic jars, beverage cases, dairy cups and tubs, food trays, pails, and oil containers. In the industry, there are constant modifications and improvements in machinery and processes. Technology is becoming an increasingly important competitive factor in productivity, as are product quality and performance. The industry is being pressed to increase the use of higher-performance polymer materials, instrumentation, controls and automated materials-handling techniques in its processing operations. While these technologies continue to be generally available, they are more demanding in their implementation, operation and maintenance, reflecting a greater need for higher levels of labour and management skills. Such skills are generally scarce. This is not so with Container Plastics.

Container Plastics is one of the few Canadian organizations that has developed extensive research and development capabilities. The Canadian market is not large. However, the free-trade agreement with United States, and the reduction in the tariff barrier that protected Canadian rigid packaging organizations, has forced Container Plastics to compete in a larger market.

In this larger market, competition is aggressive and persistent. In addition, waste disposal difficulties with plastics has placed pressure on the industry for solutions. Container Plastics and its competitors have reduced the amount of plastics used in given applications and developed means for economically recycling plastic materials. Additionally, the trade association, the Society of the Plastic Industry of Canada, has a very active program to educate the public about the role of plastics in the environment and to implement viable technologies in Canada that will reduce the amount of plastic materials that eventually reside in landfill sites.

The performance advantages of plastics over competitive products assure their status as a material of choice in a wide range of applications. Because of evolving global marketing strategies, including rationalization, and tougher competition due to lower tariffs, the industry will not maintain the past rate of growth. Nevertheless, the growth rate will continue to exceed that for the Canadian manufacturing sector.

A technological advantage of Container Plastics is that production set-up can be done relatively quickly and inexpensively. Consequently, five basic moulding machines produce nearly 100 different products. This is a sharp improvement over earlier technology which would have required 20 or more moulding machines.

Ron wants accurate product costing for profitable expansion. As the organization is new, he believes the time is appropriate for developing a costing system that is accurate and efficient. Ron has some understanding of job-order and process costing systems and standard costing, but he does not know what to use as the organization grows.

You have learned the following about Container Plastics:

- There is a sales staff of eight persons, who are located throughout Ontario, Quebec, and Northeastern United States. Agents are employed in Atlantic Canada.

- Sales persons contact clients, former clients, and prospective clients for orders. With product design engineers and the production scheduling manager, the sales person prepares a quotation.

- Generally, an order is for a certain quantity of a specified product. It will be for a future period, generally a year, with delivery being on a regular schedule or as requested if the client organization uses a JIT inventory system.

- Product pricing is a markup of 1,200 percent over cost, which is calculated as direct materials. All other costs are indirect. The markup gets reduced if necessary to obtain an order. Ron must approve all "markdowns," which he does automatically if the sales person requests.

- As long production runs reduce set-up costs, products are often inventoried for clients. There is no charge for this service.

The indirect manufacturing costs are many times larger than the materials costs, as shown below. With 27 months of data, you run simple regressions to understand what drives the various indirect cost categories. Exhibits 1 and 2 show the operating statement and the regression equations, respectively.

To maintain leading-edge technology, new equipment is constantly being considered. All proposed equipment for more than $10,000 is subject

---

EXHIBIT 1

CONTAINER PLASTICS COMPANY
Operating Statement
For the Year Ended December 31

REVENUE		$43,152,750
EXPENSES:		
Materials	4,226,740	
Machine room	15,071,788	
Warehouse	5,877,224	
Set-up	1,548,119	
Shipping	1,122,487	
Engineering	1,740,821	
Administration	1,950,298	
Selling and marketing	3,477,844	35,015,321
OPERATING INCOME		$ 8,137,429

EXHIBIT 2

Dependent Variable	Independent Variable	Constant	Slope
1. Set-up costs	Number of set-ups	$ 97,869	$2,721
2. Set-up costs	Number of orders	154,872	482
3. Warehouse costs	Square feet	769,072	7
4. Warehouse costs	Size of order	319,543	0.54
5. Shipping costs	Size of order	54,912	1.23
6. Shipping costs	Number of shipments	24,108	374
7. Machine room costs	Through-put time	671,564	119
8. Machine room costs	Machine time	974,653	197

Note: For the constant or intercept, the t-value was equal to or greater than 2 for above equations 2, 4, and 5, and less than 2 for the others. For the slope or beta, the t-value was equal to or greater than 2 for equations 1, 3, 6, and 7, and less than 2 for the others.

to capital budgeting evaluation. An example follows. Ron is concerned about whether the current approach is consistent with accepted NPV practices.

Cost of equipment	($20,000,000)
Reduction in costs ($2,500,000 per year after income taxes for the 5-year life of the equipment: $2,500,000 × 3.791)	9,478,000
Increased sales ($2,000,000 per year less 30 percent variable costs and income taxes at 40 percent for the 5-year life of the equipment: $2,000,000 × 0.7 × 0.6 × 3.791)	3,184,000
Debt financing	6,000,000
Working capital	(1,000,000)
Tax shield from equipment ($20,000,000 × 0.29)	5,800,000
Salvage value ($4,000,000 at the end of year 5: $4,000,000 × 0.3222)	1,289,000
NPV	$ 4,751,000

$$\text{Tax Shield Rate} = \frac{T \times C}{C + R} \times \frac{2 + R}{2(1 + R)}$$

where

T = the income tax rate
C = the CCA rate
R = the cost of capital or required rate of return

Required As the new controller hired to make Container Plastics a world class organization, use the case approach to put forth recommendations for a cost system that will help in accurately pricing quotations. Also, you are to make recommendations, if necessary, for improving the capital budgeting process.

Dennison Manufacturing International

"Growth opportunities are always accompanied by challenges," exclaimed the CEO of Dennison. She then went on to explain why you, a consultant, were hired.

Dennison started business in the city of Waterloo in 1951 as a manufacturer of televisions and electrical products. Television manufacturing was discontinued in the 1970s. Dennison remained in the electrical products business, which over time required it to enter many new markets. New products had to be constantly developed to maintain growth. The life of many of those products was short, and thus many products were exited after a few years. In addition, competition and the need to be cost effective obliged Dennison to locate new plants in China and India, and to enter into outsourcing arrangements. Along the way, Dennison also acquired about 30 small manufacturing plants. The result has been that Dennison now has 36 plants worldwide.

Systems integration attempts were a constant challenge because of acquisitions, outsourcing arrangements, and new product implementations. If there had been a uniform ERP system, the CEO said, there would have been fewer problems for you to resolve.

Sung, one of the older, larger divisions, has been subject to a series of problems, which the division's general manager and his controller have not been able to resolve. The CEO introduced you to the general manager and the controller. They explained that the sales have been lagging behind expectations, with the recently completed year being typical of the last three. A bigger problem has been that for the first year in decades, actual profits have become negative. You are shown the operating statement in Exhibit 1.

After a quick review of the operating statements, you asked if there have been any changes to the manufacturing process. You were told that the only change has been the use of a new supplier for the major components. The new supplier, EL

EXHIBIT 1

Sung Electronics Division
Operating Statement
For the year ending December 31
(millions of dollars)

	Budget	Actual
Sales	842.0	823.8
Variable cost:		
Direct materials, components	270.2	281.0
Direct labour	34.8	47.8
Manufacturing overhead	78.0	110.6
Selling	38.4	38.2
	421.4	477.6
Contribution margin	420.6	346.2
Fixed expenses		
Manufacturing overhead	196.4	264.4
Selling	42.4	42.2
Administration	74.4	74.6
	313.2	381.2
Net operating income	107.4	(35.0)

Sung Electronics Division
Modified Balance Sheet
As at December 31
(millions of dollars)

	Actual
Working capital	57.3
Net fixed assets	153.2
Investment	210.5
ROI, %	(16.7)

Manufacturing, was an acquisition by Dennison that occurred late in the previous year. The acquisition was premised largely on EL being able to replace most of Sung's existing suppliers. The components from EL have defects whereas the previous suppliers provided defect free components. Consequently, more materials and labour were needed, and rework and spoilage were charged to overhead.

EXHIBIT 2

Sung Electronics Division. Cost of Quality Report
For years ending December 31
(millions of dollars)

	Year T	T–1	T–2	T–3
Prevention	1.1	1.2	1.1	1.2
Appraisal	2.1	2.3	2.2	2.0
Internal failure	3.2	2.4	2.3	2.1
External failure	8.8	1.8	1.7	1.6
Total quality costs	15.2	7.7	7.3	6.9

EXHIBIT 3

Sung Electronics Division, Customer Satisfaction Survey
(percent satisfied or highly satisfied)

	Year T	T–1	T–2	T–3
Product quality	60.5	84.5	84.6	85.8
Durability	57.3	90.4	93.7	93.0
Good value	47.2	76.1	77.5	78.4
Features	61.0	69.3	70.4	70.7

EXHIBIT 4

EL Manufacturing
Operating Statement
For the year ending December 31
(millions of dollars)

	Actual
Revenue	147.4
Cost of goods sold	104.9
Gross margin	42.5
Selling and administrative expenses	36.4
Net operating income	6.1

EL Manufacturing
Modified Balance Sheet
As at December 31
(millions of dollars)

	Actual
Working capital	4.1
Net fixed assets	26.6
Investment	30.7
ROI, %	20.0

You ask for information on the cost of quality and customer satisfaction, and you receive the information shown in Exhibits 2 and 3. You are also informed by the divisional general manager that EL wants a higher price for the components being supplied to Sung. The general manager at Sung is opposed to any increase in price paid to EL because the market price is less than what EL currently charges. (You confirm with an independent source that EL is presently charging Sung five percent over the market price for the components.)

Two days later, the CEO introduces you to the general manger of EL. The financial statements for EL are contained in Exhibit 4. You learn that all of EL's production goes to Sung at a markup over costs sufficient to yield a 20 percent ROI, which is Dennison's markup for setting transfer prices between divisions. This arrangement started at the beginning of the year that just ended. The general manager of EL wants the markup to be increased in order to earn a 25 percent ROI, which he says is consistent with what is earned by other, independent firms making the same components. (You confirm that those other firms were earning 25 percent ROIs.)

Required With the case approach, respond to the CEO's assignment to resolve the outstanding issues.

CASE 12

Digital-Imaging Robots

You and your sister have a good business idea. No, upon reflection, it not a good business idea, it is a great idea. You had 15 years' experience with robotics with an automotive manufacturer. Your sister had a decade doing digital imaging research. Together the two of you have designed the next generation of industrial robots, complete with patents and firm outstanding orders for at least three years. The essence of your business model is the advanced control module that is placed in a standard robot. Money does not seem to be a problem, with all the offers from angels (rich investors who provide money and advice to start-up businesses), VCs (venture capitalists), and IPO (initial public offering) specialists.

For a start, you and your sister envisage manufacturing 10,000 robots a year in a 50,000 square foot plant in Lethbridge, Alberta. Three hundred production workers will be needed to work on two shifts. The number of maintenance employees is expected to be 50. The most important group — of engineers, programmers and systems analysts — will be those 35 involved with the research, design, development and production of the control modules for the robots. As there are a limited number of firms with advanced robotic manufacturing operations, five sales engineers will be sufficient as long as they have an equal number of support staff. Accounting and other administrative staff are expected to number 45. That set-up with improvements in productivity would allow for production to increase by 10 to 15 percent a year over a decade. Adding a third shift would increase capacity by a further 40 percent. Details are shown in Exhibit 1.

To get the business going, you have been looking for a building. There is one that appears to meet your current criteria. Your real estate agent (i.e., your mother-in-law) wants you to sign for the building before it is "off the market"; she says it is a unique opportunity. However, you are not sure about making the commitment right now, despite the agent's persistence.

The management team will be headed by you as president and chief executive officer. Your sister will be the chairperson and the vice-president of research. Two vice-presidents will need to be hired, one for production, and the other for sales. Since your wife, a chartered accountant, was just fired from her job as a tax auditor, she could be the vice-president, finance and administration, as well as the CFO. Your sister's husband, a graduate in human resources, could be the vice-president, human resources; his problem with authority figures would be unlikely to inhibit his performance.

As you and your sister work on the budget numbers for the new firm, you decide to visit the university from which you graduated in the hope of talking to one of your professors. Fortunately, he was in his office and he remembers you, and asks if you are still bullish on Dome Petroleum. (You had forgotten that recommendation. You sure believed in Jack Gallager. Too bad Dome Petroleum stock became worthless.) The office seems smaller than you remember, there are more books, but the professor, except for less hair, has changed little in 15 years. Teaching must provide a good life. You quickly explain your business plans and show him the numbers, as in Exhibit 1. Over the next hour, he asks you many questions. For some of the questions, you have answers, but for others, you do not. At 6:45 p.m., he says, "I must teach in 15 minutes. Can you and your sister meet me in my office tomorrow evening."

At the meeting on the following day, he says the following:

> Your strategy is to produce leading-edge industrial robots. Your competitive advantage is with the design stage. You are able to incorporate the latest research into the functioning of robots. However, this is but one activity in the value creation chain that leads to industrial customers that believe your robots provide advantages

EXHIBIT 1: OPERATING BUDGET, FIRST YEAR ($ MILLIONS)

	Year 1	Description
Sales	$165.00	10,000 robots times $16,500 each
Annual labour costs		
Production	$ 18.00	300 employees times $60,000
Production maintenance	3.50	50 employees times $70,000
Research and design	3.50	35 employees times $100,000
Sales — outside	0.50	5 employees times $100,000
Sales — inside	0.20	5 employees times $40,000
Accounting, administration	2.70	45 employees times $60,000
Other production costs	6.00	
	34.40	
Other annual costs		
Executives	2.00	fixed overhead
Production	10.50	variable overhead, fixed overhead
Production maintenance	5.00	variable and fixed costs
Research and design	5.00	fixed costs
Sales	1.00	variable and fixed costs
Accounting, administration	2.00	fixed costs
Building, property maintenance	0.50	50,000 square feet times $10 per square foot
Other costs	6.00	
	32.00	
Operating income	$ 98.60	
Capital assets		
Building	$ 15.50	
Production equipment	55.00	
Production maintenance equipment	10.00	
Research and design equipment	16.00	
Sales equipment	1.00	
Accounting, administration	2.00	
Leasehold improvements	6.00	
Working capital	24.00	
	$129.50	

over all competitor robots. You must design all other activities in the chain so that they too achieve world-class performance. Consider outsourcing or application service providers for those activities for which you do not have a competitive advantage. You and your sister must decide if either or both of you will be active in management, or remain as designers and owners. Also, hire employees based on merit, not family connections.

Consider your situation as a case question; and prepare for me a case response. Then I can be more explicit in addressing your proposed business undertaking.

He also provides you with information about Dell Computer, which makes extensive use of outsourcing for almost everything from sales to manufacturing, including research and development. Dell's business model invested significantly in supplier assets, which it then linked to its customer assets using the Internet and its organizational know-how and systems. Consequently, Dell enables customers to access sales and service on its website. Its network of linked suppliers makes it possible for the company to efficiently tailor PC products to fit the needs of individual buyers, whether for home use or for a global company.

He explains that Dell was quick to become Web-based for sales and customer service operations. It has no traditional distribution network standing between itself and its customers. Customers are served by a telephone or an online order taker who actually works for a division of a telephone company. More frequently, the orders are placed by the customer via Dell's Web page. Once placed by telephone or Internet, the order is sent to a co-ordinator — actually an employee who works for another company — who in turn passes the order to the relevant Dell assembly plant from among five around the world. At the same time, the co-ordinator directs the suppliers to ship the parts to the selected plant. The co-ordinator also directs the parcel courier to the respective plant at the predetermined time to pick up and then deliver the finished computer to the customer.

Moreover, Dell depends on its ability to optimize all assets that make up its business model, including relationships with employees, suppliers, investors, and customers. This clarity of business model is reflected in Dell's above-average financial performance.

Required Prepare a case response, as requested by the professor.

Dindal Air Conditioners

Dindal is a manufacturer of air conditioners for the North American market. It sells the Dindal brand through independent agents and produces units with the brand names of various retailers. Although largely an assembler of purchased parts at this time, Dindal does produce its own condensers. It also sells condensers to other manufacturers of air conditioners. Consequently, it has two operating divisions, condenser manufacturing and air conditioner assembly.

Once Dindal produced nearly all of its own components. However, over the last 20 years, it has gradually switched from making components to buying them. Now it makes only a single component, the condenser. The switching to purchased parts was done gradually. Dindal wanted to make only those parts for which it had distinct competitive and strategic advantages.

The Dindal condensers and air conditioners are durable, efficient, and competitively priced. These product characteristics have been crucial for success, and they require efficient labour, competitively priced and high-quality parts, mistake-free assembly, minimal inventories, and on-time deliveries. Also, to remain successful the condenser division has an active research and product development team that is responsible for improving the products and manufacturing processes.

Once a year, the board of directors reviews divisional performance and assesses the company's future opportunities and threats. This is an informal occasion, but the directors — especially those with significant share holdings — are very serious about understanding the operations and obtaining improved results. At this year's meeting, the directors were again unhappy with the performance of the assembly division. That division's general manager explained the poor performance as a con-sequence of the transfer price. The directors asked for a justification of the transfer price method and for regularly produced nonfinancial information on the performance of both divisions. You, as the president to whom the general managers report, have taken it upon yourself to resolve the board's concerns.

You first recognize that profitability of Dindal and its divisions has been positive and, over the last few years, largely comparable to the attached financial statements (shown in Exhibit 1 on next page) for the recent year. Each division reports as an investment centre, and the condenser division is clearly superior. Perhaps because of this unevenness of profitability, there is a dispute between the general managers of the two divisions. The condenser general manager wants a market-based transfer price. The assembly general manager wants it to be actual cost of goods sold plus 50 percent.

In reviewing the transfer price, you note that it is set at the average market price for long-term contracts to other assemblers of air conditioners. For the latest year, Dindal sold 110,000 condensers to outside customers, while the assembly division purchased 90,000 condensers. The assembly division sold 50,000 Dindal air conditioners, and 40,000 under other brand names. The bonus set by the directors last year was equal to 30 percent of a general manager's salary if their division's ROI exceeded 18 percent. The ROI is operating income divided by divisional investment. It was 35 percent for the condenser division for the latest year, but only 9.5 percent for the assembly division.

Required As the president, use the case approach and prepare a report to the board of directors, which addresses and resolves their concerns.

EXHIBIT 1

DINDAL AIR CONDITIONERS
CONDENSER DIVISION
Operating Statement
For the Year Ending December 31
(in thousands of dollars)

REVENUE		
Outside sales		$27,500
Assembly division		22,500
		50,000
VARIABLE EXPENSES		
Manufacturing	21,000	
Administration	3,000	
Selling	3,000	27,000
FIXED EXPENSES		
Manufacturing	7,000	
Selling, administration	3,000	
Research and development	2,500	12,500
OPERATING INCOME		$10,500

Division Balance Sheet

Working capital	$ 4,000
Net fixed assets	26,000
Investment	$30,000

DINDAL AIR CONDITIONERS
ASSEMBLY DIVISION
Operating Statement
For the Year Ending December 31
(in thousands of dollars)

REVENUE	
Dindal brand	$30,000
Other brands	22,000
	52,000
COST OF GOODS SOLD	31,000
GROSS MARGIN	21,000
ADMINISTRATIVE EXPENSES	7,000
SELLING EXPENSES	10,000
OPERATING INCOME	$ 4,000

Division Balance Sheet

Working capital	$ 6,000
Net fixed assets	36,000
Investment	$42,000

Do-It-Yourself Building Centres

Do-It-Yourself Building Centres (DIY) is a major regional home centre retailer with 27 stores, all located within two Canadian provinces. It competes with the market leader, Home Depot. Although Home Depot has a larger product range and lower average prices, DIY has carved out a very lucrative niche by serving homeowners who undertake renovation or construction projects.

Each DIY building centre has about 25,000 different products. A major part of its business is to provide advice to customers undertaking their own renovations and construction projects. The in-store sales associates devoted a significant part of their time to providing free advice to customers. Among other forms of advice, this involved recommending the type of paint to use on the outside of a house compared to what to use on the interior, the type of stone and patterns for an interlocking stone driveway for a suburban home, etc.

The enthusiasm of DIY to provide assistance to customers has been so prevalent that the receptionists of individual stores have been obliged to provide advice or to pass the telephone calls on to the relevant associate on the sales floors. Although providing advice had been believed to be very successful in developing a loyal customer base and contributing to profitability, the calls were frequently disruptive. Associates were often busy with in-store customers at the time of the calls. Often, the calls were put through to inappropriate associates: e.g., a paint question was given to the fence and deck associate. In addition, calls that were put on hold were frequently lost as the reception telephone systems were not designed for call centre purposes.

To more effectively respond to customer requests for information, DIY established a dedicated call centre staffed from 8 a.m. to 8 p.m., seven days a week. The call centre is located in a small town in the southern part of the region. There is a 1-800 telephone number for callers holding a valid DIY credit card to access a variety of information services. The call centre associates are equipped with a telephone and Internet access to search for information on DIY products. These associates also have access to information on the Web pages of many suppliers. All calls are recorded.

As well as getting information on store locations and opening hours, callers are able to gain free advice on products and projects. They are able to ask questions about the tools and materials for projects and to get assistance from experts with solving problems with projects they are undertaking without the need to travel to a store. All call centre associates have extensive DIY store experience, with special training in renovations and construction projects. Part of their training includes associates actually undertaking DIY projects themselves. This means they can quickly understand and effectively answer customer questions.

You are the controller for DIY. The CEO has called you into her office. She is pleased with the new call centre. The satisfaction surveys have indicated that customers are very satisfied with the call centre services. However, she wants to know if the call centre is contributing to profitability. Specifically, she is concerned about whether the callers are actually customers, if the call centre service actually contributes to sales, if the benefits exceed call centre costs, and whether call centre costs can be reduced without impairing the service. At the present time, she wants to know what information is needed to address the above concerns and how to obtain that information. The other part of the project, to be done later, will require the gathering of the information. However, for this part the requirement is merely to determine what information is to be gathered and how.

Required Use the case approach to respond to the CEO.

CASE 15

Electronic Process Equipment

Tom Simon developed a process control system in the early 1970s for an independent pulp and paper mill on Vancouver Island. He had been hired as the shift engineer, but realized that many of the operational problems at the mill could be solved with improved process controls. Although he had not set out to develop a process control system, he developed numerous individual process controls before he understood that the integration of all process controls into a system would improve the mill's operational efficiency and effectiveness. After designing and implementing the world's first integrated process control system for a pulp and paper mill, he was promoted to chief engineer. However, that did not satisfy Simon's urge to be creative.

In 1977 Simon, with two other young engineers, formed Electronic Process Equipment (EPE) to design, assemble, and implement process control systems for pulp and paper mills. Their first clients were British Columbia pulp and paper mills; then, after incorporating computers for better coordination, process control systems were sold to pulp and paper mills in Eastern Canada, to the states of Washington, Oregon, and Georgia, and to Norway. Subsequently, EPE expanded to all parts of the world where pulp and paper mills existed. By 1984, EPE was the world's leading process controls consulting engineering firm in the pulp and paper industry. The decision was made at that time to differentiate itself from all competitors by expanding into the research, development, and manufacture of leading-edge process control equipment. Then, in 1986, EPE expanded by providing process control systems to the petroleum and chemical industries.

Presently, EPE is employee-owned and highly specialized in designing and manufacturing or assembling process control equipment for customers located around the world in the pulp, paper, petroleum, and chemical industries. EPE provides a full process control service, from the initial design to the detailed engineering drawings, to the manufacture or assembly of equipment, and to its installation, testing, and ongoing maintenance.

EPE, as you would expect, has been dominated by engineers. All senior positions were occupied by engineers until 1989, when a chartered accountant was hired to be the vice-president finance. Since then there has been only one accountant among the engineers. Despite competition, EPE is now approaching annual sales of one-half billion dollars, but there have been concerns with the cost accounting system. As a consulting management accountant, you have been requested to evaluate the existing costing system and recommend changes in order that the needs of EPE be met. Your approach to the assignment is to (1) understand the existing system, (2) understand the needs for a cost accounting system, (3) understand the shortcomings of the existing system with regard to the needs, and (4) recommend a cost accounting system that meets those needs.

To understand the existing system, you meet with the vice-president finance, who (1) describes the system in general terms, (2) arranges interviews for you with the controller, manager of cost accounting, and manager of budgeting, and (3) provides you with documentation of the existing system. With these sources you piece together descriptions of the existing cost accounting system, needs, and shortcomings.

Presently, there is a distributed accounting system that is provided by the same supplier that had been used with the earlier mainframe computer. This system is adequate for valuing inventory for financial reporting purposes and for preparing periodic financial reports. It has common data and account definitions across different business units so that financial managers can readily compare and consolidate financial results across multiple units and divisions. It can prepare complete financial statements shortly after the close of an accounting period that require few, if any, post-closing adjustments. It prepares statements consistent with standards established by financial reporting, government, regulatory, and tax authorities; the system of data recording and processing has excellent integrity so that it satisfies stringent audit and internal control standards.

The existing system also reports individual product costs using variable and fixed cost classifications and responsibility centres used for external financial reporting, to value inventory and to measure cost-of-goods sold. It provides financial feedback to managers and employees on the same reporting cycle used to prepare the aggregate organizational financial statements. The chart of accounts and database capacity allows a wide variety of special reports to be produced on the same basis as the financial reports.

You interview all senior managers plus middle managers in cost accounting, sales, and manufacturing. After 13 interviews, you conclude there is unanimous agreement that the existing system is adequately meeting the requirement for financial reporting. Nevertheless, there are two shortcomings with the existing system. First, the system is inadequate in estimating the cost of activities and business processes and the cost and profitability of products, services, and customers. Second, the system is inadequate in providing useful feedback to improve processes.

The first shortcoming arises from the assignment of costs to products and services. The system uses direct labour hours to allocate indirect and support costs. Direct labour is not appropriate because direct labour is not a high proportion of the company's manufacturing conversion costs. EPE has extensive automatic manufacturing processes. It also has shifted some of the costs of materials acquisition activities (such as purchasing, receiving, inspection, handling, and storage) to a materials overhead pool; those costs are allocated to purchased items based on a percentage markup over purchase cost. To meet the needs of complex processes, multiple products and services, and diverse customers, EPE uses additional allocation bases, like material cost and machine hours. These modifications all assume that manufacturing indirect and support costs vary with the physical volume or number of the units manufactured. They fail to recognize that many expensive manufacturing resources are supplied to handle production of batches of items (activities required for set-up, ordering, receiving, moving, and inspecting products) and to design and sustain the myriad of products the plant is capable of producing (activities required to design, improve, and maintain individual products). The cost system fails to capture the economies of production batches and product variety.

Another particularly devastating loss from the inaccurate cost system is that product designers and developers receive either no information or highly distorted information about the production costs of products they are designing. EPE's costing system forces product designers and developers to use obsolete and distorted information when making design choices and trade-offs. The erroneous choices and trade-offs made during this phase become locked in; they are costly and difficult to change when the actual cost behaviour is revealed during the subsequent manufacturing phase.

The cost system relies on responsibility cost centres for accumulating costs, both primary centres where actual fabrication or assembly production work is performed, and secondary cost centres, such as indirect labour, maintenance, and tooling preparation, that provide services and support to the primary cost centres. But assigning costs to responsibility centres gives little visibility to the costs of performing activities and business processes. Most activities and business processes use resources from many different cost centres. For example, it was noticed that an activity, like *respond to customer requests,* actually involved people from seven different departments. The customer service department, where the company thought this activity was focused, incurred only about 30 percent of the total cost of performing the total activity. The lack of information about the cost of activities and business processes has impeded EPE in setting priorities for eliminating inefficiencies, and makes it essentially impossible to benchmark activity and business process costs across units, either internal or external to the organization. Consequently, EPE often does not know where to focus total quality and re-engineering initiatives.

The present cost accounting system allocates manufacturing costs to products. However, the extensive costs for marketing, selling, administration, distribution, research and development, and general administration are not assigned at all to cost objects such as products, services, and customers. This is because periodic financial reporting does not require or, in fact, allow these outlays to be assigned to cost objects. For financial reporting purposes, these cash expenditures are treated as period expenses. No attempt is made to causally link them to the activities and business processes actually being performed or to the cost objects — products, services and customers — that create the demand for or benefits from these expenditures.

As there are no financial accounting requirements at all for allocating indirect and support expenses to services produced or customers served, the service part of EPE's business does not merely suffer from distorted cost numbers; it has no cost numbers at all. There are responsibility centres for services, but there is no understanding of the costs of individual services and the costs by customer.

The second shortcoming is that the existing system does not provide adequate information to support organizational continuous learning and improvement. The present competitive environment requires managers and operators to have timely and accurate information to help them make processes more efficient and more customer-focused. The existing system prepares and issues summary financial feedback according to a monthly financial reporting cycle. Due to the complexities and adjustments associated with closing the books, the reports are delayed; though delayed only for several days after the close of the accounting period, it is still too late for responsibility centres to take immediate corrective actions. A production manager remarked:

> To understand the problem of delay and aggregated financial information, you could think of the responsibility centre manager as a bowler, throwing a ball at pins every minute. But we don't let the bowler see how many pins he has knocked down with each throw. At the end of the month we close the books, calculate the total number of pins knocked down during the month, compare this total with a standard, and report the total and the variance back to the bowler. If the total number is below standard, we ask the bowler for an

explanation and encourage him to do better next period. We are beginning to understand that we won't turn out many world-class bowlers with this type of reporting system.

In addition, the monthly performance reports for many operating departments contain extensive cost allocations, forcing managers to be held accountable for performance that is neither under their control nor traceable to them. The costs of corporate- or manufacturing-level resources, such as the heat and lighting in the building or the landscaping outside, are allocated arbitrarily to individual departments despite the departments having no responsibility for these costs. For example, referring back to the bowling metaphor, think about the accountants, after a ball is thrown down each of the establishment's 35 lanes, counting every pin knocked down, dividing by 35, and reporting back the average (say, 8.25714) to every bowler. The number may be quite accurate (it does represent the mean number of pins knocked down per alley), but it is completely useless to an individual bowler. Each bowler wants to know the number of pins he or she has knocked down in order to improve on the next throw. A number has no value when it is influenced by actions of others who are uncontrollable.

Required Recommend a cost accounting system that meets the needs of EPE. Explain and justify your recommendation.

Foodco Limited

As a leading Canadian integrated restaurant company with seven branded restaurant chains, Foodco has in the last five years completed acquisitions of various small restaurant chains. In the most recent year, acquisitions of restaurants accounted for 14 percent of the system growth. Existing restaurants only delivered two percent growth. The board of directors wants future growth to come from existing brands. In addition to top line or sales growth, the board of directors wants to reduce costs. They suggested a company wide cost reduction initiative.

Foodco was established in 1883. It went through many changes to where it is now — one of Canada's largest restaurant firms. The seven operating chains or brands are as follows:

- Chicken Chalet, family/casual restaurant chain specializing in rotisserie chicken and barbecued ribs.

- Manny's, quick service restaurant chain serving hamburgers.

- Betty's Neighbourhood Bar & Grill, casual dining that provides guests with an innovative, varied menu featuring a fun environment.

- Dakota's Cookhouse, providing young families with fun, value and genuine hospitality featuring comfort foods in a wilderness lodge setting.

- Overland Steakhouse, casual dining featuring seasoned steaks, fresh fish, etc.

- Good Cup, leading specialty coffee retailer delivering superior quality, service excellence and coffee passion.

- Millstone Grill & Bar, casual upscale dining that provides guests with familiar food and beverages.

Foodco's strategies for growth are straightforward:

- Lever brands
- Drive geographic expansion
- Maximize supply chain leverage
- Increase organizational effectiveness
- Develop human resources.

A major component of these strategies is to examine existing chains to identify opportunities to improve cost effectiveness.

You have met with the general managers for seven restaurant chains to introduce each of them to the cost-reduction project established by the board of directors to reduce costs. The basic information is available with Exhibits 1 to 7. In your discussions you wanted to understand the differences for sales and earnings, specifically between "company owned and managed" restaurants and those that are franchisee-managed and sometimes franchisee-owned. You learn that franchisees invest their own money, which allows Foodco to finance more rapid growth.

You also learn from the general managers that the non-company-owned restaurants are less successful as their levels of sales and earnings per store are usually less than with "company owned and managed" units. Franchisees, it was explained, are less willing to adopt the latest practices learned by the "company owned and managed" restaurants. When you ask for evidence of this sub-optimal performance, the general managers say that information is not systematically produced. Nevertheless, they all agree that non-company-owned and -managed restaurants have inferior performance.

Foodco has joined a group of owners of restaurant chains, which has hired a consulting firm to benchmark the performance of restaurants. The project was started during last year, and consequently only sales and earnings (before amortization of property, plant and equipment and interest expenses) benchmarks are available by restaurant type. (Note: Consulting firms often approach companies to establish industry performance standards. Each of these companies submits its financial information to the consulting firms, which develop benchmarks for the various types of industry. The information submitted by each company is kept confidential, but the consulting firms are able to present benchmarks as external performance standards. This generally would create a desire among the participants, individually or in group, to hire these consulting firms to benchmark their performance.)

The consulting firm was able to analyze the performance of Foodco chains to determine whether "company owned and managed" restaurants were superior to the franchised restaurants. The consulting firm reported that there was not much difference between the performance means (sales and earnings) of the two types of restaurants. How-

---

EXHIBIT 1: CONSOLIDATED STATEMENT OF EARNINGS ($ MILLIONS)

	Year T	T–1
Systems sales*	2,400	2,105
Gross Revenue*	1,530	1,411
Earnings before the following	175	148
Amortization of property, plant and equipment	66	57
Interest expenses	9	7
Earnings before income taxes	100	84
Provision for income taxes	30	25
Net income	70	59

* Revenue recognition: Gross revenues include revenues from Foodco owned and operated foodservice activities. These activities consist primarily of food and beverage sales. System sales includes gross revenues as noted, together with the revenue from all franchised activities.

EXHIBIT 2: CONSOLIDATED BALANCE SHEET ($ MILLIONS)

	Year T	T–1
Assets		
Current Assets		
Cash	101	91
Accounts receivable	51	69
Inventories	28	29
Other current assets	18	15
	198	204
Property, Plant and Equipment	418	389
Goodwill	49	49
Brands and Other Intangible Assets	175	120
	840	762
Liabilities		
Current Liabilities		
Bankers' acceptances	32	52
Accounts payable, etc.	145	133
	177	185
Long-Term Debt	202	160
Other Long-Term Liabilities, etc.	83	66
	285	226
	462	411
Shareholders' Equity		
Capital Stock	33	31
Retained earnings	345	320
	378	351
	840	762

EXHIBIT 3: SYSTEM SALES AND GROSS REVENUE BY BRAND ($ MILLIONS)

	Year T		T–1	
	System Sales	**Gross Revenue**	**System Sales**	**Gross Revenue**
Chicken Chalet	740	393	704	393
Manny's	482	212	457	234
Betty's	371	268	322	243
Dakota's	222	191	151	118
Overland	75	75	62	62
Good Cup	312	155	238	176
Millstone	280	280	204	204
Interdivisional	(82)	(44)	(33)	(19)
Total	2,400	1,530	2,105	1,411

EXHIBIT 4: EARNINGS* BY BRAND ($ MILLIONS)

	Year T	**T-1**
Chicken Chalet	71	66
Manny's	43	35
Betty's	38	33
Dakota's	8	3
Overland	3	3
Good Cup	6	3
Millstone	11	8
Interdivisional	(5)	(3)
Total	175	148

*Earnings before amortization of property, plant and equipment and interest expenses.

EXHIBIT 5: SAME RESTAURANT SALES GROWTH (PERCENT)

	Chicken Chalet	**Manny's**	**Betty's**	**Dakota's**	**Overland**	**Good Cup**	**Millstone's**
Year T	1.2	1.8	(0.2)	0.7	(6.0)	(0.3)	3.1
T–1	2.7	3.0	0.8	(2.4)	(4.7)	4.0	0.8

EXHIBIT 6: BENCHMARK RESULTS PER RESTAURANT

	Sales, $ millions		**Earnings*, % of sales**	
	Foodco Unit	**Benchmark**	**Foodco Unit**	**Benchmark**
Chicken Chalet	3.96	3.50	9.6	8.7
Manny's	1.37	1.10	8.9	8.4
Betty's	3.34	3.00	10.2	8.6
Dakota's	4.15	3.90	3.6	8.3
Overland	4.69	6.50	0.4	8.5
Good Cup	0.82	1.10	1.9	7.9
Millstone	12.2	15.00	3.9	8.9

* Earnings before amortization of property, plant and equipment and interest expenses.

EXHIBIT 7: RESTAURANTS BY TYPE OF OWNERSHIP

	Company Owned and Managed	Owned and Franchisee Managed	Franchisee Owned and Managed	Total
Chicken Chalet	50	74	63	187
Manny's	58	125	168	351
Betty's	67		44	111
Dakota's	38		16	54
Overland	16			16
Good Cup	20	7	355	382
Millstone	23			23
Total	272	206	646	1,124

ever, it noted that the variance was very large for these chains. There were a relatively large number of poorly performing restaurants among "company owned and franchisee managed" and "franchisee owned and managed" restaurants. Equally, there were a large number of exceptionally well-managed restaurants, with above-average performance.

Required You, the manager of management accounting, have been asked to scope out the project for reducing costs. Use the case approach to respond to the board of directors.

French Oven Restaurants

Established 10 years ago, French Oven operates 51 family-style restaurants in the Lower Mainland of British Columbia. All restaurants have the same menus and adhere to the same practices. The intent is to consistently create high quality food and service. To further ensure consistent and high quality food, the company recently established a central kitchen or plant to produce about 30 pre-prepared servings for the French Oven Restaurants. The plant is also expected to produce servings for institutions such as hospitals.

The plant accountant has started to develop a costing system, but the president did not approve it. As the management accountant for the company, you have been asked by the president to suggest alternative cost systems for the plant. Of the alternatives, you are to recommend the costing system that you deem to be the most appropriate for the plant. You are to use the case approach.

The plant produces individual frozen meals that can be quickly prepared and served. These individual meals are produced in batches that are stored frozen in the warehouse until shipment to a French Oven restaurant or an institutional customer. Meals are prepared from recipes on a production line that has, depending on the item, as many as 16 stages or channels. Exhibit 1 shows the channels, while an example of a recipe is shown in Exhibit 2.

Production passes through the required channels. The elements of cost are: raw materials, ingredients, packaging, labour, overhead and warehousing. The costs of raw materials, ingredients and packaging are calculated by the use of a recipe sheet — e.g., Exhibit 2 — which is really a bill of materials for a batch of one of the 30 different products. For costing purposes, the recipes are input into a computerized program called Recipe Master List. All costs are calculated on a hundred weight (CWT) basis. Instead of this system, raw materials (red meats and poultry) are costed with a manual system.

EXHIBIT 1: CHANNELS	
Code	**Activity**
110	Spice room
120	Butcher shop
130	Pan/stuffing
140	Bake/roast
150	Meat/broth
160	Cooking kettles
170	Frying
180	Slicing
190	Trim
510	Weigh
520	Pop-out
530	Sure flow
540	Bulk pack
550	Salad dressing
560	Case packing
6410	Warehouse

The actual costs of the component items are updated frequently on the Inventory Master Listing. At the same time, the updated costs are input to the Recipe Master List. This permits the timely revision of the costs of the finished products.

The costs of ingredients and packaging also appear on another report, the Product Rate Master. The ingredients are indicated by the 200 series of the expense codes and the packaging items by the 400 series. This list also contains labour and overhead costs, listed by channel code.

Direct labour dollars are applied to production at each channel the product batch passes through. A labour grid is prepared for each product. This grid lists the various channels for the product and the number of workers required to staff each channel. The worker classifications and the hourly rates are used to calculate a weighted-average cost per hour for direct labour.

EXHIBIT 2: RECIPE, MEAT LOAF WITH BROWN GRAVY EXAMPLE, PER BATCH OF 100 SERVINGS

Product: 20023

Stock no.	Description	Quantity (kg)	Price/kg ($)
21009	Beef 85 percent	50.00	2.00
21011	Beef 50 percent	20.00	1.75
61275	Catsup	1.50	1.00
61073	Bread crumbs	3.50	0.75
61072	Crouton crumbs	4.00	1.40
21005	Meat loaf ends	5.25	0.95
61375	Dry onions	4.00	0.75
61093	Celery stock and leaves	6.00	0.95
61545	Salt	1.00	1.90
61445	White pepper	1.00	2.25
31014	Frozen eggs	4.50	1.25

Next, a standard kilograms of product processed per hour is developed for each channel. A weighted average of the actual production runs expected to come from the prior year is used for this calculation. The direct labour cost per CWT is recorded on the Product Rate Master report by channel and is indicated by expense code. These costs become the basis for the assignment of overhead.

The budgeted direct labour dollars for the warehouse are divided by the forecasted quantity of production (cases). The result is the warehousing cost per case, with the accompanying overhead costs also allocated on a per case basis.

The following overhead rates are developed for each of the 16 channels in the plant. Each of these overhead rates is expected to be based on costs from the current year's budget. The overall rates are applied to direct labour dollars. The methods used in calculating each rate are as follows:

- **Burden — labour (setup costs).** Setup labour is to be allocated to each channel based upon the previous year's actual costs. These costs are divided by the budgeted direct labour dollars for each channel to arrive at the burden-labour rate per direct labour dollar.

- **Burden — other (plant costs).** The current year's budgeted amounts for the following costs are included in the overhead allocation to burden — other: indirect labour, cleaning labour, maintenance labour, fringe benefits (on above labour), natural gas, electricity, small equipment, and channel supplies. The overhead rate for burden

— other — is calculated by dividing these costs by the budgeted direct labour dollars for each channel.

- **Fringe benefits.** Vacation and holiday pay, payroll taxes, pension costs and health insurance costs are included in fringe benefits. A rate of fringe benefits cost per hourly payroll dollar is used to determine the cost of fringe benefits for direct labour and set-up costs. The cost allocated by this method is then used to develop an overhead rate based on the direct labour dollars.

- **General plant overall (GPO).** Costs of an administrative nature are included in GPO. At the plant, the items in Exhibit 3 are included in plant overhead. The total of these costs is divided by the direct labour dollars to determine the GPO rate.

- **Amortization, taxes and insurance (ATI).** The amortization expense of major pieces of equipment is allocated to the channel where they are located. The balance of the equipment amortization and all of the building amortization are allocated to each channel based on the square footage each occupies. Taxes and insurance are also allocated to the channels on a square footage basis. The total of the ATI costs for each channel is divided by the budgeted direct labour dollars for that channel to develop the overhead rates.

The various elements of costs are summarized and updated in a report called the Cost Rate Maintenance Report.

EXHIBIT 3: GENERAL PLANT OVERHEAD

- salaried labour and fringe benefits,
- laundry and gloves,
- paper, laboratory and cleaning supplies,
- fuel oil (for the office),
- water softener supplies,
- sewer and septic,
- garbage,
- outdated stock,
- repairs and maintenance,
- telephone and Internet,
- postage and office supplies,
- PCs and supplies,
- travel expenses,
- employees' services expenses,
- experimental expenses,
- dues and subscription, and
- equipment rentals.

- **Raw material rate.** The total of the calculation of raw materials costs is used for this rate.

- **Ingredient rate.** The ingredient costs are totalled for this rate.

- **Direct manufacturing expense (ME) rate.** The costs of direct labour, packaging, burden (labour), burden (other), and fringe benefits are included in this rate.

- **General Facilities rate.** The costs of the GPO and ATI are included in this rate.

The Cost Rate Maintenance Report is the basis for costing the finished production each month. The quantities of each item produced during the month are multiplied by the four cost rates, and a total standard cost of each is listed at the end of the production report. This total is debited to finished stock inventory each month.

Products are made, as mentioned, in batches. For each batch, the actual costs are compared to the standard costs. Variance analysis at the batch level is intended for the plant supervisor to assist them with making daily adjustments to improve efficiency and effectiveness.

Required   Undertake the assigned project with the case approach.

Fusion Computing Inc.

Fusion Computing Inc. is a two-year-old firm that has been growing rapidly through new product development and geographical expansion. The first budget was completed about nine months ago. Presently, the second budget cycle starts in a month. Now the CEO is reviewing the earlier experience in an attempt to make improvements to the budgeting process. You have been hired on a three-month contract to review the budgeting process, recommend changes to the board, and assist with the implementation of the next budget.

Substantial importance is placed on budgeting. Specifically, Fusion's strategic plans are implemented with the budgets. The goals and objectives of the strategic plans are budgeted or quantified and expressed as commitments. The acquisitions and use of resources are also explicitly budgeted. The budgets are, therefore, commitments to financial forecasts and agreements on expected outcomes.

Like any other planning activity, budgeting at Fusion helps managers focus on one direction chosen from many future alternatives. The CEO with other members of senior management defines the chosen path using some accounting measure of financial performance, such as net income, earnings per share, or sales level in dollars or units. Budgeting is the tool, at Fusion, that managers are to use to successfully plan and manage operations and programs. Accounting based measures provide specific quantitative criteria against which future performance (also recorded in accounting terms) can be compared. Budgets are used as a standard for accessing actual performance.

Budgets were used to help identify potential problems in achieving specified goals and objectives. For the 12 month horizon, the managers in charge of responsibility centre budgets were expected to consider all possible events that might affect budgeted performance.

The results of the first budget are shown in the attached operating statement (see Exhibit 1) for the first nine months of this year. Currently, it

EXHIBIT 1

Fusion Computing, Inc.
Operating Statement, Total Corporation,
For the nine months ending September 30 of this year
($ 000s)

	Actual	Budget	Variance
Sales	479,326	525,000	45,674 U
Cost of goods sold	321,669	300,000	21,669 U
Gross margin	157,657	225,000	67,343 U
Period cost:			
Sales	87,543	85,000	2,543 U
Administration	35,860	35,000	860 U
Research	67,159	40,000	27,159 U
Other	17,537	10,000	7,537 U
	208,099	170,000	38,099 U
Operating income	(50,442)	55,000	105,442 U

is October 5. Fusion has a board of directors, a CEO and five vice-presidents. Two vice-presidents are responsible for product manufacturing. There is a vice-president for sales, another for research, and a fifth for finance and administration. The latter vice-president is responsible for financial accounting, budgeting, treasury, and other administration matters.

To carry out your assignment, you review the budgeting process from last year. It started on November 1. The management group (the five vice-presidents and the CEO) reviewed the budget submission during the first week of January. Some of the budgets had to be reworked before the management group met for the second time during the third week of January to approve the budget. The board met twice in February to approve the budget, which everyone agreed was highly satisfactory. Finally the January to December budget was implemented last March 1, two months after the current year began.

You interviewed the five vice-presidents individually. Four of them supported the budgeting. Improvements were suggested.

One of the production vice-presidents said she was pleased to see the CEO actively involved, but noted he had a limited amount of time. As a result, the communication of basic process information was frequently overlooked, resulting in the need for revisions relatively late in the process. She prepared only one budget for her entire area, with the result that there was high unfavourable budget variance.

The other production vice-president said he had substantial difficulty in budgeting as the sales vice-president was very vague about the sales to be accomplished. In the end, he had to guess as to the sales and to create a production budget for that level of sales. He also said that as sales from his production plant were greater than the original budget, he should not be evaluated against the original budget. He prepared budgets for the eight responsibility centres for which he was responsible. These eight responsibility centres rolled up to the consolidated budget for all of his responsibilities.

The sales vice-president was concerned that the fixed 12 months for the budget would prevent her from preparing for emerging opportunities and threats beyond the original December year end. The firm was in dynamic businesses subject to significant changes.

The vice-president of finance and human resources advised you to talk directly to the controller and the treasurer, who were the two managers most involved with the administration of budgeting. The controller prepared the entire budget except for the cash budget. He said the process was evolving, and steps and procedures were becoming clearer to all involved. The controller had worked closely with the two production vice-presidents and the sales vice-president to ensure that the sales budgets were consistent with production budgets and that direct labour, direct materials, and overhead were consistently budgeted.

As Fusion was new to budgeting, there were many mistakes. The treasurer had difficulties with planning the receipt and payment schedules for accounts receivable and accounts payable. This was a result of the company having no experience on which to base the accounts receivable and accounts payable. The original cash budget proved useless, but continued to be used. Consequently, bank loans were used, and sometimes they were used when there was surplus cash.

The vice-president of research refused to participate in the budgeting; he claimed that budgeting would inhibit research creativity. The CEO prepared the budget for research.

Required As the consultant, use the case approach to make recommendations for improving the budgeting process at Fusion Computing Inc.

CASE 19

Government Services

You are the newly appointed deputy minister of a provincial government department. There are 6,000 employees in the department, grouped into a corporate office plus six regions. Each region has a regional director. The corporate office has 400 employees who provide policy development and centralized services.

Each region is an autonomous unit run by a powerful regional director. The power is in terms of certain political and community support. The minister and his cabinet colleagues want these regional empires reduced in power and brought under your control. There have been problems because the regions have been delivering programs according to the regional directors' wishes, rather than as legislated.

When you explain to the regional directors what you want done in the way of program standardization, they all agree, but nothing changes. You cannot terminate these regional directors because they have many years of service with performance evaluated at excellent for all recent years. The process of documenting poor perfor-

mance, and by that terminating regional directors, would take years. These regional directors are all well paid, and unlikely to leave on their own. The story circulating is that they do not need to change because you will soon leave, just like your predecessors.

You have a problem. You have promised the minister and the premier that you will standardize program delivery, but the regional directors who must do it for you will not co-operate. You have one year, or be terminated. As an "order-in-council" appointee, the minister can terminate you on short notice. However, you cannot terminate the regional directors in the same way as they are appointees of the public service commission. You are at a loss for a solution. Responsibility accounting does not seem to work.

Required   With the case approach, put forth alternatives, evaluate their likelihood of success, select the most appropriate, and then suggest an implementation plan.

Harry Rosen

Last Tuesday morning you went with your boss to a breakfast meeting sponsored by the Society of Management Accountants of Ontario. The purpose of the meeting was for CMAs (like your boss) to encourage prospective new members such as yourself to become CMAs. To encourage a turnout, there was a speaker, Mr. Larry Rosen, the CEO and president of Harry Rosen Inc.

Larry started with the following statement:

We don't perceive ourselves as being in the clothing business. We don't just sell suits and sport jackets. It's a relationship-based business. My business is to get to know you, to have you build a relationship with one of my highly trained associates. I want to be your clothier for life. The whole key to our business is loyal clients. I strongly believe we have a corporate culture that has a love of quality and a love of clients. And building customer relationships is a managed process.

Larry's opening comments made you think of what you had read the previous night when you had googled "Harry Rosen."

The company Harry Rosen was started 54 years ago by Harry Rosen the father of Larry Rosen.
— *Website for Harry Rosen Inc.*

Harry Rosen Inc., a retailer of some of the most powerful brands in quality menswear, has built itself into a powerful national brand. That brand is based not simply on what it sells — because styles and designers change and fall in and out of fashion — but in how it sells. The brand provides a service promise to its customers, and this promise has been used effectively as a marketing and sales strategy to communicate the company's value proposition.
— *The Deloitte perspective*

The Harry Rosen chain is using [customer relationship management] technology the way it's supposed to be used, by creating an electronic concierge. What the company has been able to do is take what Larry Rosen's father used to do personally for a much smaller client base and use technology to do the same thing for a much larger one.
— *Ken Wong, associate professor of business and marketing strategy Queen's School of Business*

You have known Harry Rosen Inc. as an upscale men's clothing retailer with a relentless focus on the customer experience. You did not think you were old enough, as you had always considered Harry Rosen Inc. to be an "old man's" clothier. However, with Larry's statistics that the average customer was male and 39 years old, you now think you may have been wrong, and perhaps you are ready to be a Harry Rosen Inc. customer.

Larry spent about 45 minutes describing his company. It had been established by his father Harry and his uncle Lou in the Kensington Market area of Toronto with just $500 in start-up capital. Although men's wear was, and remains, a highly competitive business, Harry managed to make his firm stand out by establishing it in the minds of customers as a place where they could get their fashion questions answered. Larry said men are reluctant shoppers, and thus helping men purchase clothing was the way in which the company created a relationship. The focus of the relationship between associates (sales employees) of Harry Rosen Inc. and customers was on creating a confident image for aspiring customers. The relationship was developed through advice, trust, and continuity.

EXHIBIT 1: HARRY ROSEN ADVERTISEMENT

POSITION:

Shoe Specialist Associates (Full Time)

REPORTS TO:

Store Manager

LOCATIONS:

Sherway Gardens, Etobicoke, ON
and Yorkdale Shopping Centre,
Toronto, ON

MAIN RESPONSIBILITIES:

- To achieve and exceed sales and productivity standards
- Clientele development with respect to relationship selling in the Shoe Department
- Assisting in the maintenance of the Harry Rosen store image, in the Shoe Department and Stockroom inventory management
- Providing superior standards of service to all customers
- Provide feedback regarding Shoe Assortment and Selection
- Support with the Marketing and Product Knowledge Training

QUALIFICATIONS:

- Strong commitment to achieving excellence in the area of customer service
- Strong interpersonal skills
- Strong communication skills
- Professional attitude and appearance
- Footwear experience in retail/high-end sales preferred

Harry Rosen Inc. has luxury stores. Presently, there are 16 stores across Canada and 700 employees. Traditional financial performance measures, such as sales growth and profitability, are important. Information technology is also important at Harry Rosen Inc. for two reasons. First, executives and buyers at Harry Rosen use data-analysis tools from Cognos Inc. built into a GERS Inc. merchandising system. The system offers more than a dozen sales and inventory reports for analyzing sales and helps the company identify sales trends, manage inventory, and calculate gross profit margins. Second, Harry Rosen Inc. uses information technology to maintain detailed customer information to better serve customers.

Harry Rosen Inc. has managed to become a household name in Canada, partly through the use of creative advertising to promote awareness and to cultivate a luxury image. One recent example is the company's teaming up with the Princess Margaret Hospital to promote a charity run for prostate cancer treatment. This has created substantial positive exposure in the Toronto market. There are plans to expand this charity run to other Canadian cities.

Larry Rosen also mentioned that the company hires for attitude and trains for skills. The advertisement depicted in Exhibit 1 attests to the importance of attitude and skills.

After Larry Rosen's presentation, you and your boss talked to him about the use of management accounting. Larry Rosen said that the management accountants were considering implementing a balanced scorecard. Your boss said that you had developed a balanced scorecard. Larry Rosen asked you what you would suggest for Harry Rosen Inc. in the way of a balanced scorecard.

Required Using the case approach, develop a balanced scorecard for Harry Rosen Inc.

Home Renovations

You have just become a shareholder of Home Renovations, Inc. Of the outstanding shares you own 10 percent, while Jean Paul Flynn, the founder, owns the remaining 90 percent. Mr. Flynn started Home Renovations 20 years ago with only himself. Now there are 15 permanent salaried employees, plus 200 to 300 trades persons on contract for 20 or more hours a week.

You are also the chief financial officer, controller, and office manager. You manage the 5 office staff, while Mr. Flynn manages the 10 estimators/project managers.

There is a strong demand for renovations. However, new firms are capturing most of this growth. Mr. Flynn suspects internal problems as the cause of Home Renovations not capturing its share of this growth. However, he is unsure about the problems and their resolution. He has allowed you to buy into the organization in the expectation that you will identify and solve the problems.

You devoted your first month to understanding the organization. The following paragraphs summarize your initial findings.

Homeowners generate renovation business by requesting an estimate for some renovation work. Examples would be a new roof, an external extension, rooms in the basement, and a wooden deck. Mr. Flynn sends an estimator/project manager at the first mutually convenient time. This meeting leads to a written quotation for the renovation, which is usually in competition with other renovators. If the quotation is successful, Mr. Flynn assigns the first available estimator/project manager. That estimator/project manager will hire the trades persons, such as plumbers, carpenters, cement makers, insulators, drywallers, and electricians for the various components of the project. The estimator/project manager will order the materials, which he will deliver or arrange for the vendor to deliver to the job.

Estimators/project managers are generally skilled in two trades, plus experienced in estimating projects and managing them to completion. In this dual role, they estimate the likely cost of renovation projects and manage renovation projects. The dual role ensures high utilization of time. Managing projects is a means of basing estimates on a thorough understanding of actual projects.

Renovation projects average $15,000. The average project requires a lapsed time of five weeks from start to completion, and three trades persons. Quotations would include a 20 percent markup for overhead and the project manager's time. Thus, the $15,000 job would be $12,500 for trades and materials plus 20 percent or $2,500.

Almost all the jobs are completed on time, but half exceed the cost estimate. When the project manager tries to collect on cost overruns, the customer often is reluctant to pay the extra. Generally only 20 percent of the overruns are collected. The remainder is written off. Last year these overruns reduced the operating income by half. Moreover, the request for additional money creates ill will and reduces repeat business.

You investigated the last 160 jobs, and found that 75 of them had overruns. Of the 75, 70 were where the person who managed the project was not the original estimator. Also, you noticed that all overruns were because of trade costs. There were no material overruns.

As you preceded with the investigation, you asked all estimators/project managers why they had overruns. Their explanations were that the projects were incorrectly estimated. They said the projects could not be completed within the cost estimate. Similarly, you asked each estimator/project manager why others were not able to bring their estimated projects to completion within the cost estimate. Their answers were that the other estimator/project managers did not always expect much from the trades when someone else estimated the project.

You then reviewed the process used for contracting trades. The office staff maintains a list of trades available for work. The system is based on trade type and equality. For each trade there is list, and the listed names are organized according to order of registering. When, for example, a cement maker is needed, the first name is chosen. If that person is not available, the name is placed at the end of the list (after the third "unavailable," a name is dropped). If available, the trades person is used, and his/her name is placed at the end of the list.

When assigned, the estimator/project manager tells the trades person what must be done and the completion date for key aspects of the project. A trades person usually works on two or three projects at Home Renovations simultaneously. This is necessary to average 20 hours of work or more per week. Weekly hours will vary with the number of active trades persons on the lists.

The monthly financial statements are based on GAAP. Revenues are estimated based on the percentage of completed contracts, less incurred materials, trades, and period expenses, which include salaries and wages. The latter include all 15 employees, plus Mr. Flynn and yourself. The accountant calculates the profitability of each project at the end of the year. This helps with reassessing the markup for fixed overhead and profits.

Required Using the case approach, prepare a report to Mr. Flynn analyzing the problems at Home Renovations and the recommendations that will resolve them.

Inner Streets Youth Drama Association

Seven years ago, Jean Nadeau formed Inner Streets Youth Drama Association (ISYDA) to help runaway and homeless youth to leave the downtown streets of a large western Canadian city. These young people have run away from home and dropped out of school. From the ages of 12 to 22, they are occupied with alcohol, drugs, petty crime, and prostitution. They are split almost evenly between males and females, and about 60 percent have at least some Native background. Most have no regular place to stay at night.

Jean had a similar background but had managed to leave the streets and get an education: first a bachelor's, then a master's degree in education. Despite having natural teaching abilities and a very high grade point average, Jean never became a teacher. Instead, he started ISYDA, with little financial support.

ISYDA believes that the problems of street kids are the result of painful experiences and low self-esteem. It also believes that these problems are solvable through self-expression and by taking charge of one's life. Drama is a vehicle for self-expression, and so ISYDA started drama groups in downtown social agencies frequented by the street youth. The youth developed skits and plays depicting their lives and problems. Through discussion among themselves and with audiences, they gained greater understanding of themselves, their families and their friends. ISYDA also started preventative programs in several junior and senior high schools where there were youth at risk of street lives. In these school programs, participants were referred by teachers. Referrals also came from fellow students. Community groups around the province began to request ISYDA plays and workshops and other sessions on how to develop similar drama programs.

ISYDA participants develop the plays themselves, with Jean or other facilitators helping in the process. Their drama concerns included such issues as drugs, prostitution on the streets and AIDS.

ISYDA also has a residential program because participants in the drama programs often have no place to stay. The association rented a large house for sub-lease to some youth. It is for short-term accommodation for youth on social assistance. They pay for rent and food. Jean lives in the house, but the youth make the rules.

By teaching the youth to understand themselves and their situation, drama acted as a means of getting them off the streets. This worked in two ways. First, while in the group, they were off the street, at least temporarily. Second, the therapy achieved through drama helped them to resolve many of their issues, and so they became able to pursue off-the-streets alternatives, such as attending school, returning home, or obtaining employment. Due to its success in getting a significant number of young people off the streets either temporarily or permanently, ISYDA also became successful at raising funds for operations and capital expenditures.

There are five sources of funds. The first source is foundations that have in their mandates the support of social service activities such as ISYDA. This source supplies start-up or special undertakings, such as drama tours or drama camps. There is a limit to the number of years a group receives funding from this type of source. During ISYDA's middle years, it was the most important source of funds.

The second source is ongoing operational funding. This comes from several agencies funded by the government, and this funding signifies an acceptance of the importance and effectiveness of an agency. About two years ago, ISYDA began receiving this funding for about half its operating costs; this is currently its largest source of funding.

The third source is federal and provincial employment grants, at minimum wage rates. This was the most important source of funds in the first few years of ISYDA; then the grants paid Jean and the facilitators. More lately, they pay youth to obtain work skills.

Fourth, performances and workshops generate money. ISYDA, the youth performers, and support staff share this money. Some years, depending on the particular plays and talents of the actors, this has been as much as 20 percent of total revenues.

The last source is donations. This can come from individuals or groups. For example, a local technical college repaired extensively a $1,000, 15-person van for the wholesale cost of parts. A service club denoted the other van. (ISYDA records the market value of donations as revenue.)

ISYDA is a dynamic organization, carrying on a multitude of flexible programs that respond to the youth clients and their circumstances. Each program constitutes an organizational unit or responsibility centre. Each program has a set of definite expectations, e.g., method of operation, number of clients, and client progress by period. It is the organizational formulation of these expectations for helping street youth that entices support from funding agencies.

Jean sees the structure capturing the special attributes of ISYDA, as noted in the chart in Exhibit 1.

ISYDA has been successful both with helping street youth and with raising funds. Exhibit 2 shows the expenditures for the latest year. Jean is the only full-time employee. He hires part-time facilitators and administrators as needed. The focus is on helping the clients and not on a permanent organization. It is crucial to avoid deficits.

Each program has detailed and accurate records as funding agencies require feedback on

how their monies were spent and with what results (i.e., the number of youth helped). The youth are readily identifiable by program, and so is the funding. However, expenditures can be direct or indirect. The direct costs are the hours an employee devotes to a program as a proportion of his or her work day times total remuneration. Other direct costs would include materials, any monies paid to the youth for performances or practices, and snacks. (Provision of snacks has always been a component of programs, as many youth are living in atypical settings. They often come to practices and performances hungry. The snack may include a restaurant meal when on tour — i.e., McDonalds — but most often includes the purchase of food to prepare sandwiches or even a hot meal.)

Indirect costs are more difficult to allocate, and some are even joint. Gasoline and other transportation costs are usually difficult to allocate, but the travel record could be used to allocate them to programs. Each travelled kilometre relates to a program.

You have recently joined the board of directors as the (volunteer) treasurer. In the meetings you have had with the board, funding agencies, and Jean, there have been suggestions that there are shortcomings with the accounting information. An executive director of one of the larger funding agencies put the problem succinctly when she said, "We provide ISYDA with money, but we are not sure where the money goes. Sure, for the programs we are funding, we get client numbers and their progress. We appreciate this. However, we would like to know how the money is spent within the

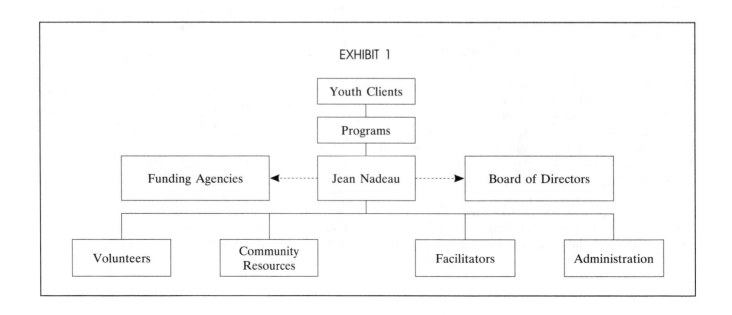

EXHIBIT 1

EXHIBIT 2

INNER STREETS YOUTH DRAMA ASSOCIATION
Income Statement
For the Year Ended December 31

	Year T	T–1	T–2
REVENUES			
Government funding	$ 60,000	$ —	$ —
Foundation grants	22,000	42,000	21,000
Performance, workshop	10,905	9,652	9,876
Employment grants	7,305	17,854	10,554
Rent	5,400	1,700	—
Donations	6,940	21,893	2,575
Total	112,550	93,099	44,005
EXPENSES			
Salaries, benefits	33,100	30,600	20,000
Contract employee payments	27,500	25,500	9,500
Transportation	24,250	21,200	9,000
Snacks	3,200	2,500	3,500
Rent on house	11,100	4,900	—
House utilities, repairs	3,500	1,900	—
Food at house	4,200	1,500	—
Administration	5,100	4,400	2,300
Total	111,950	92,500	44,300
NET REVENUE	$ 600	$ 599	$ (295)

INNER STREETS YOUTH DRAMA ASSOCIATION
Balance Sheet
As of December 31

	Year T	T–1	T–2
ASSETS			
Cash	$10,050	$ 5,000	$ 1,000
Accounts receivable	9,450	10,000	8,000
Inventory, supplies	150	100	50
Prepaid rent	900	900	—
Fixed assets, vehicles, net	20,500	15,500	1,000
Total	$41,050	$31,500	$10,050
LIABILITIES			
Accounts payable	$ 1,500	$ 2,000	$ 1,000
Unearned revenue	38,146	28,696	8,845
SURPLUS (DEFICIT)			
Accrued to current year	804	205	500
For 1992	600	599	(295)
Total	$41,050	$31,500	$10,050

programs we fund." ISYDA submits financial statements for the total organization to all funding agencies. Sometimes this pacifies them, but some request more specific information, which requires hurried projects for allocating costs to individual programs or sub-programs.

With this concern in mind, you review the accounting system with Jean and a volunteer who inputs the financial transaction data with a computer accounting package. The accounting format is for a single entity. Nevertheless, the package being used has the capacity to report revenues and expenses for 10 programs plus consolidating. Exhibit 2 shows the financial statements for ISYDA.

You note that there are nine different programs, as shown below:

- Riverbend Community Centre
- J.J. Laurier Drop-in Shelter
- Southwest High School
- Southwest Junior High School
- Crump Junior and Senior High School
- Northern Tour
- Central Tour
- Summer Camp
- House

Required The board of directors asked you to address the concerns of the funding agencies for regularly produced accounting information by program. Be specific regarding individual expenditures and accounting practices, and use the case approach.

CASE 23

King Coal

The provincial government's electrical utility has a coal mine in the King region that produces thermal and metallurgical coal using an integrated pit mine and cleaning plant. Separate reporting is not done for the extraction and cleaning plant or for the thermal coal and metallurgical coal. The assumption is that if the total cost is competitive, then each part must be efficient. Although this may have been a reasonable approximation in the past, new mines have been opened that are more efficient. Now the utility's senior management wants to manage the cost of each part individually.

The controller has assigned you to calculate the profitability of the operations. The reason for your assignment is to figure out, as accurately as possible, the exact costs of each coal (thermal and metallurgical) and each operation (extraction and cleaning) at the King Mine. Then you are to compare the costs with other operations of the utility and with industry averages. These costs will be the starting points for specifying annual improvements in productivity and cost effectiveness. A component of this study will be to devise a transfer price between the extraction and cleaning plant, if that would motivate cost effectiveness. When he assigned the project, the controller conveyed the transfer price idea of a board member, but admitted he does not understand why it would be beneficial. The controller asks that you explain transfer pricing and its possible benefits in your report.

The production process includes the extraction and hauling of raw coal to the cleaning plant. The cleaning plant prepares both types of coal for shipment by rail, the thermal to a thermal plant and the metallurgical to a private steel mill.

The financial performances of the extraction and cleaning operations, and the ancillary support and administrative activities combine into a single operating statement. The statement is shown in Exhibit 1. You realize that to accomplish your project you will need to allocate these costs to the two coals and two operations. Subsequently, you

arrange appointments with managers and other employees who are knowledgeable concerning the content and drivers for each expense line item.

Employees are transported by company bus from two towns where they live to the mine site. The last 27 kilometres into the mine is a company-maintained road.

You find that the annual contract for thermal coal is 450,000 tonnes, and 150,000 tonnes for metallurgical coal. For each contract, King mine is the prime supplier, and the customers make up any shortage by alternative and more expensive secondary suppliers. The mine ships the full amount for contract each year. The metallurgical coal generates revenue at the rate of $78 per tonne. The thermal coal does not generate revenue because it is shipped to a thermal plant owned by the provincial government. To estimate a transfer price, you ask the general manager for the thermal plant what would be the landed cost of thermal coal on a long-term contract. She estimated the cost to be $71 per tonne (delivered) for comparable coal. The traffic officer (responsible for arranging for and monitoring transportation) explained that King ships clean coal at the cost of $6 a tonne.

The mine is a series of interlinked pit mines that produce 652,000 tonnes per year. Excavation equipment and trucks remove the overburden. The pits differ by coal type, and for efficiency purposes the miners extract thermal coal for three weeks, and then metallurgical coal in the fourth. Pit mining wages and benefits, amortization for pit trucks and equipment, and depletion costs are entirely attributable to the extraction of the coal. These costs are the same per tonne for both thermal and metallurgical coal.

Shrinkage in the cleaning plant through the elimination of impurities reduces the weight by eight percent. The expenses for the cleaning plant include plant wages and benefits and amortization for plant and equipment. The metallurgical process has additional stages and, thus, a higher cost per tonne than thermal coal. You estimate that

EXHIBIT 1

KING MINE DIVISION
Operating Statement
For the Year Ending December 31
(in thousands of dollars)

REVENUE
    Thermal coal $ —
    Metallurgical coal   11,700

EXPENSES
Extraction wages and benefits	$10,500	
Plant wages and benefits	9,500	*— cleaning plant exp. < 70% th. / 30% Met.*
Diesel fuel, gasoline	3,800	
Amortization, pit trucks, equipment*	3,000	*— extraction*
Amortization, buses*	900	
Amortization, plant equipment*	2,800	*—> same for both coals, extract.*
Amortization, costs	800	
Management salaries and benefits	2,700	
Administration	2,300	
Facilities, utilities and taxes	2,600	
Marketing department	800	39,700
Net income before income taxes		$(28,000)

* Amortization is based on the physical exhaustion of the asset

70 percent of all cleaning costs are attributable to thermal coal, and 30 percent to metallurgical coal.

Diesel fuel and gasoline expenses track to tank locations and invoiced prices. You estimate that $3,500,000 was for extraction, $150,000 was for the loaders in the plant, and $150,000 was for the buses.

There are nine buses scheduled to drive back and forth between the two towns and the mine site where all employees report for work; 500,000 kilometres were driven last year. Employees take the bus about 98 percent of the time. The following table shows the breakdown of employees by department:

Extraction	41%
Plant	26
Management	13
Administration	15
Marketing	5

When analyzed according to where they work or how they devote their average work day, the management, administration, and marketing personnel had the following to say in aggregate:

	Extraction	Plant	Neither	Total
Management	45	35	20	100%
Administration	45	40	15	100%
Marketing	—	—	100	100%

joint cost

About $600,000 of the administration expense item is attributable to buses. Square feet occupied is the cost driver for facilities, utilities and municipal taxes. You calculate the allocation to be 45 percent for extraction, 35 percent for plant, 10 percent for administration, 5 percent for management, and 5 percent for marketing.

Required Complete your assignment using the case approach.

Major Electronics

Major Electronics is a multi-plant assembler of computers and computer products. It has 40 plants located in southern Ontario and greater Montreal. In recent years, there have been concerns that its traditional method for allocating manufacturing overhead (MOH) is no longer relevant. Direct labour costs now average 6 percent of manufacturing costs for its 40 plants, with 55 percent for direct materials, and 39 percent for manufacturing overhead.

The corporate management accounting branch is investigating alternative cost drivers. MOH is divided into three groups: procurement, production, and support. The standard chart of accounts for Major further classifies these costs into sub-classes (see Exhibit 1), which are ranked in order of importance.

The corporate management accounting branch surveyed manufacturing managers at all 40 plants to obtain a list of the most important cost drivers for MOH. With these cost drivers, an analysis was done to ascertain their correlation coefficient (r) with MOH in total and each of the three major groups. Each r is shown in Exhibit 2.

These results were presented to a group of plant managers that was formed to provide advice to the corporate management accounting branch on the development of alternative cost drivers. The committee was not surprised at the correlations. However, they had two concerns that could not be immediately resolved. First, the committee was unclear about how a positive r in regression analysis implied that the respective costs were driven by a cost driver. With regression analysis, there is a constant (or alpha or intercept) and a slope (or beta). The slope coefficient is comparable to variable costs per unit of the cost driver. The constant is comparable to the fixed costs. Many members of the advisory group were puzzled about whether total indirect costs from a pool should be allocated, or just the variable costs. Second, some overhead costs have been incurred for capacities much greater than current production. For example, in most plants the materials specifications units

---

EXHIBIT 1: SUB-CLASSIFICATION OF MANUFACTURING OVERHEAD COSTS

Procurement	Production	Support
• Stores	• Direct labour payroll taxes and benefits	• Production engineering
• Purchasing	• Occupancy	• Process engineering
• Materials	• Direct labour supervision	• Manufacturing management
• Engineering	• Other indirect labour	• Quality assurance
• Materials management	• Operating expenses	
• Production control	• Amortization	
• Material specification	• Production management	
• Inbound freight	• Equipment expenses	
• Traffic and receiving	• Shipping	
• Corporate materials charges		

EXHIBIT 2

Cost Driver	Total MOH	Procurement	Production	Support
Total manufacturing space	0.57	0.32	0.50	0.49
Average total head-count in manufacturing	0.86	0.44	0.81	0.56
Direct labour dollars	0.73	0.12	0.77	0.45
Direct material dollars	−0.17	−0.12	−0.44	−0.30
Number of part numbers	0.13	0.45	0.16	−0.06
Percent of parts inspected on receipt	0.00	0.24	−0.11	0.16
Number of products	0.53	0.19	0.50	0.59
Number of customer orders per month	−0.05	−0.04	−0.07	0.08
Average cycle time in days	0.10	−0.21	0.19	0.21

operate at 50 percent of their full capacity. Many members thought underutilized capacity should not be allocated to existing products. It was thought that this would not be fair when facing competitors that were operating at full capacity.

Required   As the project manager for the alternative cost drivers project, prepare a report using the case approach that makes recommendations for a successful project.

Modern Chair

You have just started working for Modern Chair, a new organization that uses a modern, automated approach to the manufacture of a variety of chairs. Using computer-assisted design specifying and ordering materials and scheduling manual and machine activities, every chair can be unique, and Modern Chair can offer individual design on demand. Modern controls costs, which are lower than those of competitors who have less automation and less ability to efficiently produce small batches. Nevertheless, the success of the company has led to a problem. Currently, with the economy in what looks to be a temporary boom, there is a shortage of capacity. There are no plans to expand production capacity to meet temporary excess demand. The president asked you for recommendations for making the best use of limited production capacity. Your recommendations are to facilitate profit maximization.

In your investigation, you realize that there is not much in the way of information on which to base the recommendations. The organization has little history, and the president has personally made all important decisions. You note, however, that besides the design department that has unlimited capacity, there are two production departments: the first department assembles the chairs, while the second does the finishing. Although there are 252 different types of chairs if all styles and finishes are considered, Modern divides them into two types, upholstered and straight back. Using this conceptualization, you allocate production costs according to assembly or finishing. Within each department, you further divide the costs according to upholstered or straight back chairs.

Then you take the cost for each product category in each department and run simple regressions, and get the results seen in Exhibit 1.

Each department's total available hours are 3,920 hours a year, i.e., 16 hours a day for five days a week for 49 weeks a year. The assembly department runs five identical lines. The yearly capacity is 19,600 operating hours. The finishing department runs four lines for 15,680 hours of available time. An average upholstered chair sells for $147 and the average straight back chair sells for $76. Sales of straight back chairs are unlikely to exceed 25,000 at that price, while that price will restrict upholstered chairs to 25,000. There is sufficient capacity in the assembly department, but not in the finishing department.

For each department, the standard hours in production needed to produce the chairs are as follows:

	Upholstered	Straight Back
Assembly	0.75	0.50
Finishing	0.45	0.75

Modern occupied its current facilities four years ago. The assembly department cost $927,000 for plant and equipment. The finishing department's plant and equipment cost $554,000. About 80 percent was for equipment, while the remaining 20 percent was for the land and buildings. Since then, the capacities of the two departments have increased about five or six percent a year. The managers and employees found ways to increase efficiency and effectiveness.

In examining the non-manufacturing costs, you find that they are all fixed except the five percent sales commission paid on the sales price of each chair.

Required You have just finished a nice lunch at Spartan's and are seeing the President of Modern Chair within an hour. Linear programming comes to your mind as being a suitable tool. What analysis and recommendation would you provide? Use the case approach.

EXHIBIT 1

Variable	Coefficient	Standard Error
ASSEMBLY DEPARTMENT		
With the total costs of upholstered chairs as the dependent variable		
1. Constant	$ 98,747	$246,868
Independent variable: Time in production hours	$27.14	$11.81
$r^2 = 0.55$		
2. Constant	$352,363	$167,922
Independent variable: Direct labour hours	$11.74	$10.67
$r^2 = 0.33$		
With the total costs of straight back chairs as the dependent variable		
1. Constant	$347,428	$386,031
Independent variable: Time in production hours	$21.11	$ 6.60
$r^2 = 0.61$		
2. Constant	$797,318	$346,660
Independent variable: Direct labour hours	$ 5.06	$ 5.62
$r^2 = 0.35$		
FINISHING DEPARTMENT		
With the total costs of upholstered chairs as the dependent variable		
1. Constant	$ 27,957	$ 8,223
Independent variable: Time in production hours	$ 4.74	$ 1.16
$r^2 = 0.67$		
2. Constant	$ 54,819	$ 10,542
Independent variable: Direct labour hours	$ 3.51	$11.70
$r^2 = 0.31$		
With the total costs of straight back chairs as the dependent variable		
1. Constant	$155,850	$141,682
Independent variable: Time in production hours	$ 6.18	$ 1.29
$r^2 = 0.50$		
2. Constant	$347,310	$ 86,828
Independent variable: Direct labour hours	$ 3.57	$ 2.75
$r^2 = 0.33$		

CASE 26

Pasta, etc. Family Restaurants

You are a member of an independent consulting firm that specializes in serving the restaurant industry. Unlike many consulting firms that are extensions of audit firms, your firm has serious and in depth expertise with the restaurant industry. The following is a typical assignment.

"Pasta, etc." is a chain of Italian casual dining restaurants located in southern Ontario. The restaurants are at the top end of the casual dining segment; guests are offered many of the benefits of fine dining without the formality. The menu is limited to approximately 20 entrees to ensure a high level of execution and service. Menu items such as steaks, pork chops, ribs, roast beef, chicken, seafood and salads are complemented by a wide assortment of alcoholic and other beverages.

The chain is only five years old, but already there are 74 outlets. The owners had planned to expand the number of outlets to 100 in Ontario over the next two years and then expand across Canada and into the United States. However, recent performance has been disappointing.

Some background is useful. The Torra family arrived in Toronto from Italy in 1955. Tony worked in an Italian restaurant immediately upon arrival in Canada. After one year he started his own restaurant, which provided him and Enza and their two children with a very good livelihood. Both boys — Joe and Donnie — went to university. Joe became a high school mathematics teacher, while Donnie became a dietician and joined the family restaurant.

As the original restaurant was not large enough for Tony and Enza, plus Donnie with his growing family, Donnie persuaded the other members of the family that expansion was necessary. It took three years to convert the original restaurant into an expansionary "model restaurant" that would be relatively simple and, therefore, could be managed by a non-family member.

The excitement of expanding the family business encouraged Joe to give up teaching high school mathematics in order to return to the family business. In the following five years, Joe and Donnie went from one to the current 74 restaurants. They are now wondering what happened.

All 74 restaurants are basically the same. Sales have exceeded expectations, but profits are much less than expected. There is some variability in sales among the 74 restaurants. There is a scheduling model that, based on sales, assigns the optimal number of employees to be on staff for each restaurant (i.e., restaurants with higher revenue will require more employees in order to maintain service quality). The planning, budgeting, and financial reporting systems are fully adequate. Employees are remunerated with basic wages, plus incentives tied to sales. These incentives account for about 20 percent of the average employee's remuneration, and thus there is a keenness among employees to maximize sales.

In your consulting assignment, your concern is with what is going wrong with the restaurants. You suspect operational problems; thus, you and your associates study a random sample of 5 of the 74 restaurants. All five are very similar, with the restaurant in Exhibit 1 being representative.

Because Joe and Donnie cannot agree on the reasons for the profit shortcomings, and thereby on the solutions, your consulting firm has been hired. Joe believes that sales improvements will solve the profit shortcomings. Donnie, in contrast, believes the inadequate cost control has caused the profit shortcomings. However, neither has been able to gather convincing evidence.

Pasta, etc. is fortunate in having a specialized restaurant enterprise resource planning (ERP) system that has the potential for linking all systems. Although the potential of the ERP system is just starting to be utilized, it can calculate the price and variable costs for the 20 entrees that are being sold. This information is shown in Exhibit 2.

EXHIBIT 1: OPERATING STATEMENT ($ 000s)

	Budget	Actual
Sales	$2,900	3,060
Variable cost of sales		
Direct materials	500	713
Direct labour	900	1,126
Variable overhead	200	257
	1,600	2,096
Contribution margin	1,300	964
Fixed costs		
Other labour	150	152
Rent	200	197
Utilities	150	157
Miscellaneous	50	46
	550	552
Net Income	750	412

Required Use the case approach to identify and solve the profit problems facing the model restaurant.

EXHIBIT 2: PRICE AND VARIABLE COST PER ENTREE

	Price Per Entree	Variable Costs per Entree
# 1	$27.50	$20.25
# 2	24.75	18.05
# 3	24.00	15.24
# 4	19.75	13.04
# 5	19.50	8.39
# 6	17.50	7.90
# 7	12.00	6.59
# 8	11.25	7.88
# 9	19.75	9.94
#10	8.50	4.09
#11	13.00	9.44
#12	21.50	13.74
#13	17.25	9.86
#14	14.00	8.23
#15	20.50	13.75
#16	18.00	6.71
#17	14.50	7.62
#18	10.00	4.85
#19	14.50	7.42
#20	19.75	10.67

PC-Board

PC-Board Limited is a leading North American manufacturer of advanced printed circuit structures used in a variety of complex electronic applications. The company markets its products to major original equipment manufacturers (OEMs) and large contract assemblers in the telecommunications, computer, automotive, and industrial electronics industries. For example, the company currently manufactures printed circuits for the latest generation of high-speed fibre optic switching stations, wireless communication sets, laptop computers, bar code reading systems, and electronic engine-control assemblies.

In recent years, there was significant investment in new manufacturing systems. In the past five years alone, the company invested more than $50 million in the most advanced manufacturing technology. Future investments are expected to be about $5 million per year for further automation of operations and the introduction of new processes.

Investment growth has been paralleled with enhancements to employee training and product quality. The company's commitment to human resource development includes continuous resource development, training, and re-skilling. The company's culture of quality, teamwork, and continuous learning was reinforced by an annual average of 80 hours of classroom and on-the-job training per employee.

The company's human resource and quality investments have been recognized. PC-Board's three plants satisfied the stringent requirements of the international standard for quality assurance management systems, and obtained the ISO 9002 official registration from the Quality Management Institute. The company's major suppliers of primary materials and components also allowed their quality processes to be audited according to the ISO 9002 standards.

Price increases are not expected from year to year, nor does the current business plan factor in any forecasted improvement in market conditions. The company is committed to internal improvements as a basis for sustained profit improvements. However, it will be possible to obtain higher average prices, through an improved product mix featuring a greater proportion of higher value-added products.

Accordingly, the most significant challenge is to further increase productivity as measured by the reduction of manufacturing cycle times. The manufacturing strategy is to optimize learning and, therefore, slide down the cost curves with the new technologies developed with customers.

PC-Board is dominated by engineers and marketers. The president, an electrical engineer, was advised by the external auditor to hire a controller who could develop management accounting systems that would be appropriate and cost effective. You are that controller, and you report to the president. Previously your position, up to a year ago when you joined the company, reported to the vice-president of marketing, and it was called the chief accountant.

Your present task is to review and make recommendations for the cost accounting system, which evolved with the last three chief accountants. Basically, the cost accounting system keeps track of the costs for producing an order. An order may take a few weeks or months to produce, and accounting reports are produced at regular intervals. Each order is made with selected operations undertaken by specialized capital equipment operated by skilled employees. Although the orders differ, each product in a particular order will receive exactly identical amounts of the company's resources.

The cost accounting system compiles the costs by order. Direct materials and purchased components are charged to the order. Conversion cost (indirect costs and labour cost) are charged for each operation based on the time in production and other cost drivers. Actual conversion costs are charged to orders; however, the operations are well understood so that standard conversion costs could be used.

After examining the cost accounting system, the following recording practices are typical of what is employed for each order.

Materials, components inventories	XXX	
Accounts payable, cash		XXX
Work in process, operation 1	YYY	
Materials, components inventories control, conversion costs allocated		YYY
Work in process, operation 1	ZZZ	
Conversion costs allocated		ZZZ
.		
.		
.		
Work in process, operation 9	VVV	
Conversion costs allocated		VVV
Finished goods	SSS	
Work in process		SSS
Cost of goods sold	PPP	
Finished goods		PPP

After your review, you discuss the accounting system with members of the accounting department. They believe the accounting system to be accurate, but they are concerned that the reports are not used regularly by the manufacturing and marketing departments. The newly promoted assistant controller expressed the frustration of the accounting department when she said, "We prepare timely and accurate reports on each operation in the sequence of producing an order, but not a single person cares."

The company is always trying to reduce costs; thus, with the cost accounting reports not being used, you wonder if they can be replaced with something less expensive. You then visit the manufacturing and marketing departments, and interview the 12 persons that receive the reports. The conclusion from these interviews is that these manufacturing and marketing decision-makers only want the final cost of an order. At the end of the interview, the vice-president of manufacturing left you with the following assessment: "The accountants mean well with their detailed costs accounting by operation, but it is of no use to us. The money it costs for 90 percent of those reports is wasted."

The president also wants you to examine a recurring problem with the company's bidding process for new orders. As each order tends to be large, all senior managers are involved with the submission of bids. The accounting department constantly disagrees with the manufacturing department on bidding decisions. Typically, the company wants to earn a 30 percent profit margin on total

costs, which both departments accept, however they disagree on some individual bids.

You examine the accounting department practices in costing bids. The department costs a possible order by including: materials, purchased components, and indirect costs. No direct labour is added as all labour is considered fixed. Thus, labour and other indirect costs are allocated with the most appropriate cost drivers. For example, set-up costs are allocated based on the number of set-ups, inspection by the number of inspections, assembly by the throughput time, etc.

The accountants use an ABC system. Costs are assigned to activities based on use of resources, then assigned to cost objects, such as products, based on the use of activities. Six assumptions underlie the use of ABC. First, activities consume resources, and acquiring resources creates cost. Second, products or customers consume activities. A third assumption is that ABC models consumption rather than spending. This assumption's implication is perhaps the most important. For costs to decrease, there must be a change in spending. ABC, however, does not measure spending — it measures consumption. In the short run, a change in activity will have little or no impact on the consumption of resources. In the longer run, adjustments can be made to bring spending into alignment with consumption.

The fourth assumption, closely related to the first two, is that there are numerous causes for the consumption of resources. A further assumption, implicit in the fourth assumption, is that a wide array of activities can be identified and measured. These activities serve as linkages between the costs of resources and cost objects. The linkages enable multiple cost pools rather than a single cost pool to be used — reflecting a cause-and-effect relationship. A major advantage of ABC is the recognition that the activity measures can be organized into a hierarchy, namely:

- Unit-level activities, which are performed each time a unit is produced,

- batch-level activities, which are performed each time a batch of goods is produced,

- product-level activities, which are performed as needed to support the production of each different type of product, and

- facility-level activities, which simply sustain a facility's general manufacturing process.

A fifth assumption of ABC is that cost pools are homogeneous, which means that for each cost pool there is only one activity. The implication is that there are many cost pools. The sixth and last assumption of ABC is that all costs in each pool are variable (strictly proportional to activity). When this assumption is coupled with the previous assumption of cost pool homogeneity, it becomes apparent that only costs considered "fixed" in the traditional sense would be "facility-level" activities.

The vice-president of manufacturing admits to the conflict that his department has with the accounting department. He is frustrated in not being able to reconcile what he believes with what the accounting department believes. This was less serious, he said, before the firm implemented ABC. In discussing the conflict with the vice-president of manufacturing, you realize that he views costs much differently than the accounting department. First, he is concerned with throughput contribution, which he defines as revenue minus the variable cost of materials, purchased components, and energy. He believes that all other costs are fixed, e.g., indirect manufacturing costs and all labour. Second, optimal performance to him is to maximize the throughput contribution. To maximize throughput, the vice-president is constantly eliminating or attempting to eliminate bottlenecks to allow production capacity to increase. For example, the vice-president removed a bottleneck with two machines in the group producing the fibre optic switching stations. These machines were bottlenecks, as they were operating at full capacity while other machines in the sequence were operating with unused capacity levels. The solution was to reduce the load of the bottleneck machines by shifting operations performed onto other machines. This increased total capacity for fibre optic switching stations by 12 percent.

Nearly all orders are obtained by winning bids, even with long-term clients. Orders vary in size from $2 to $40 million, with most in the $20 to $30 million range. The bidding committee consists of the president, the five vice-presidents, and you, the controller. In effect, the bidding committee is a formal means of working with the vice-president of marketing in her submission of bids. The committee ensures that all bids are appropri-

ately priced and that, if successful, the conditions of all bids are met.

In analyzing bids, the accountants cost the potential order by adding the actual costs of materials and purchased components to the cost of the required operations at the allocation rates established by ABC. A 30 percent markup is added to these costs to cover other overhead and profits. You, the controller, generally vote in favour of bids prepared by the vice-president of marketing when the price equals or exceeds the cost plus the 30 percent markup.

The manufacturing department analyzes all bids with throughput contribution. All bids and potential bids are ranked as to their total throughput contribution and according to the ratio of the throughput contribution to total variable cost of materials, purchased components, and energy.

Generally, there is agreement on about 80 percent of the bids. The accounting department generally rejects the remaining 20 percent because the markup is less than the 30 percent. Manufacturing generally votes in favour of these additional orders on the basis that those bids are competitive and that there is capacity to produce the orders. Moreover, the vice-president of manufacturing says, "If there are more orders, manufacturing is forced to find ways to increase capacity by eliminating bottlenecks. This increased capacity provides a larger base to allocate fixed costs." You believe the vice-president of manufacturing is sincere in what he believes, but now you are unsure how it can be reconciled with the ABC that your department uses with bids. However, you are going to have to reconcile the two systems for the president.

Required Complete the assignments for the president. Be sure to explain why there is a conflict between the manufacturing and accounting departments, and provide recommendations for resolving the conflict so that the bidding committee can make the best short-run and long-run decisions for PC-Board.

Persaud Products Company

You are the vice-president of manufacturing for the Persaud Products Company, which makes products for wireless communications. The majority owners started the company to manufacture products based on their inventions and patents. The company has grown rapidly over its three years of existence.

The company consists of five departments: human resources (HR), manufacturing, research, sales, and finance and administration. Manufacturing uses the latest equipment, systems, and technology to produce the products invented by the research department.

In the last few years the company has increasingly formalized its management systems. For example, the department heads of the HR, manufacturing, and research have co-operated to develop techniques to measure and forecast performance. The department heads for sales and finance and administration have developed a budgeting system. The new budgeting system, however, has made your department (manufacturing) look unfavourable.

Units within the HR, manufacturing, and research departments have set longer-term, aggregate goals based on benchmarked performance measures such as return on capital. The elements or factors measured are key performance indicators (KPIs) such as profits, cash flows, cost ratios, customer satisfaction, quality, and time to market. The performance criteria for benchmarking are the performance of internal or external peer groups and the results from in prior periods. In addition, the company's units in HR, manufacturing and research departments are measured and rewarded on the basis of how well they reduce fixed costs and improve uptime (e.g., the time that a piece of equipment is working — the opposite of down time) in comparison to best-in-class industry benchmarks.

Empowerment has been expanded. Employees are free to make mistakes and equally free to fix them. Managers have significant discretion in making decisions. Consequently managers can obtain resources more quickly than in traditional companies and without the need for elaborate documentation, partly because they are accountable for the profitability of their units and can, therefore, be expected to shed any excess expenses in the event that demand falls. In such a system, the "spend it or lose it" creed that is at work in traditional units has no meaning.

The KPIs tend to be financial at the top of the department and more operational the nearer the unit is to the front line. It has been found that KPIs do not need to be precise to be effective.

Rolling forecasts for the next 12 months play an important role. The forecasts, generated each month, help managers to continuously reassess current action plans as market and economic conditions change.

The budgeting system is even newer than the company. Budgeting has been done for two years. The budgets are expected to be prepared on an annual basis and detailed first by quarter and then by months within those quarters. Budgeting is started in October and completed by December 10 or prior to the commencement of the new fiscal year on January 1. Participation is emphasized throughout the budgeting process until the budget is approved by the president and CEO, Kim Persaud, who is also in charge of sales. Kim approves the master budget herself before submitting it to the board for final approval. Thus, the final budget omits approval by the heads of departments such as manufacturing (yourself), HR, research, finance and administration.

With the assistance of the latest software, the 12 month budget is prepared. At the end of each month, one month is deleted and another is added. The forecasts assist with assessing the next 12 months. This allows the company to pursue continuous budgeting. Thus, Persaud Products is always budgeting 12 months into the future. This continuous budgeting has become the integral planning and control device for achieving two strategic

EXHIBIT 1:   OPERATING STATEMENT, MANUFACTURING DEPARTMENT
FOR THE MONTH ENDING MARCH 31 ($ 000s)

	Actual	Budget	Variance
Variable costs:			
Direct materials	$ 4,576	$ 4,027	549 U
Direct labour	2,924	2,489	435 U
Variable overhead	3,707	3,114	593 U
	$11,207	$ 9,630	1,577 U
Fixed costs:			
Supervisor and manager salaries	$ 1,389	$ 1,400	11 F
Facilities	890	900	10 F
Equipment	765	800	35 F
Other fixed expenses	496	500	4 F
	$ 3,540	$ 3,600	60 F
Total	$14,747	$13,230	1,517 U

objectives: ongoing new product development, and rapid continuous improvement.

After the budget is approved by the board of directors and implemented, it becomes the standard against which performance can be measured. This is accepted by all managers in all areas; i.e., they know that their performance will be evaluated by comparing actual results to budgeted results. Despite this understanding, you and your boss, Kim Persaud, have a disagreement on your department's performance during the last month.

In reporting to the board of directors for the first quarter, the CEO praised her own sales efforts for being 20 percent over the sales budget of $25,000,000. In front of the board Kim criticized you for being $1.5 million over your budget (see Exhibit 1). You did not say anything at the time. Your manufacturing budget of $13,230,000 was established to accomplish the sales budget of $25,000,000, and you believe that your department exercised effective cost control. All sales were made at the budgeted prices, and all variable costs were transacted at budgeted prices and rates.

Required Using the case approach, respond to the CEO explaining the performance of the manufacturing department during the last month. Be sure to include suggestions for improving the budgeting process and the use of budgets by managers.

Precious Metals

Just after their December examinations, four management accounting students, who had been team members in a management accounting course, met to consider an equity investment. A relative — a young mining engineer — had asked one member to evaluate a mining proposal, offering him the opportunity to become a shareholder.

This new venture was to mine precious metal on a property that had in the past been considered to have too small of an ore body to be economically viable. Located about 500 kilometres north of Toronto, the mine in question is close to good roads. Moreover, as there is substantial unemployment in the area from the closure of other mines, appropriately skilled workers, with an expected average wage of $22 per hour, are plentiful. Five years ago, when unemployment levels in the province were low, an average wage of $25 might not have attracted the required labour force.

Recent changes in the technology of mining equipment have made economical the mining of smaller properties. Diamond drilling surveying was done for the property's ore body. The survey concluded that the property has sufficient ore for a mine and processing plant operating for 20 years at 1,500,000 tonnes (1 tonne = 1,000 kilograms) per year. The expected yield is 0.05 percent; i.e., for every tonne there will be 0.5 kilograms of the precious metal.

The mining engineer estimated the equipment and plant at $38 million. Of the total assets, half has a CCA rate of 30 percent, one third has a CCA rate of 20 percent, and the remaining one sixth has a CCA rate of 10 percent. The assets will last for the life of the ore body, after which time the expected salvage value is $2 million; only assets subject to 30 percent CCA are salvageable.

The estimated processing costs (excluding amortization or capital cost allowance) are $16 a tonne. Estimated administrative and selling costs are $4 million and $1 million per year, respectively. Working capital requirements are $1 million. An added initial investment of $1 million will recover other trace minerals. This would amount to 100,000 kilograms a year at 10 percent of the kilogram price of the precious metal. Operating costs and other costs would increase by 10 cents a tonne. There is no expected salvage value for these assets, which are in the 30 percent CCA class.

The mining engineer has spent $100,000 for the property, diamond drilling, incorporation, and solicitation for investors. The company must reimburse her upon start-up. She is also considering the idea of asking $5 million for the company.

The price per kilogram of the precious metal is likely to fluctuate because the metal is a material for luxury goods that varies in demand and price directly with the North American economy. A consulting economist used probability analysis to present estimates of future prices:

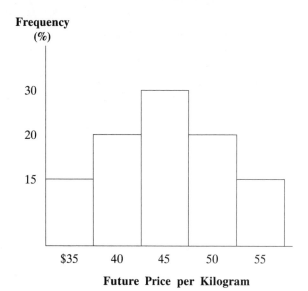

Future Price per Kilogram

Precious Metals would be a typical mining company. Its key success factors would be market price for the metal, yield of the ore, and operating costs per tonne of ore.

There is to be a board of directors to whom the general manager (i.e., the young mining engineer) would report. This board would need to approve the 20-year plan. The board also approves the annual budget and reviews the quarterly performance in comparison to the budget. Otherwise, the general manager has complete autonomy in managing the mine.

The team members have two other concerns: (1) the risk inherent in fluctuations, and (2) that the young mining engineer will run the mine for her benefit and not the owners'. You and your team members had a long discussion about how the owners could be assured that she made decisions best for the company and not just herself. While the team members believed her to be honest, they all believed that differences in objectives could put the interests of the investors in jeopardy.

The discount rate (R) is 8 percent after tax. The income tax (T) rate is 40 percent. Calculate the tax shield with the following equation (C is the CCA rate). For the first year, the half-year rule applies, and it is shown as the second part of the equation.

$$\text{Tax Shield Rate} = \frac{T \times C}{C + R} \times \frac{2 + R}{2(1 + R)}$$

Required

Use the case approach to

1. Evaluate the investment opportunity with a discounted cash flow technique.
2. How would you control the costs in developing the property for production so that the objectives of the owners are being incorporated into decisions and actions?
3. How would you control the general manager after the start of production so that the objectives of the owners are being incorporated into decisions and actions?

Royal Trust

Required You just joined a major stock broker-age firm. As a condition of your employment contract, you were hired as a research analyst with duties to analyze companies and make recommendations as to whether the shares of certain companies should be bought, held, or sold. Your contract also specified that after one year of experience with the firm, you would become the analyst responsible for banks and financial institutions. On the first day, the director of research asked you to use past annual reports and stock price patterns to explain, with the case analysis approach, the 1993 demise of Royal Trust. He explained that Royal Trust had been a very successful firm over most of its long life, but in a relatively short period of time it ran into problems that were not satisfactorily resolved.

You start by gathering together the Royal Trust annual reports for the 1983 to 1992 period, along with monthly stock prices.

The Royal Trust Company ceased operations in 1993. The Royal Bank, an unrelated company, purchased its trust operations and the name Royal Trust; the remaining assets were placed in a new firm called Gentra Inc. This was the end of a 94-year life for Royal Trust; it was also the end of a 10-year period where Trilon Financial Corporation, a financial holding company, was the major shareholder.

In 1983, Trilon Financial Corporation came to own, directly and indirectly, just over 50 percent of the shares of Royal Trust. Upon acquiring majority ownership of Royal Trust, Trilon installed a new chairman, Mr. J. Trevor Eyton, and a new president and chief executive officer, Mr. Michael Cornelissen.

Chairman Eyton announced two new committees in his 1983 annual report message to shareholders, in addition to the "usual complement of board of directors' committees." The first was the business conduct review committee, which was charged with preparing and monitoring an updated code of business conduct, reviewing business ethics within the company, and resolving any conflict of interest situations applicable to employees, directors, and major shareholders. The directors on this committee were to be independent of the major shareholders, Trilon. The second committee was the investment review committee, which was to consist of seven directors, with the majority being "unaffiliated shareholders directors." The duties of this committee included the review of investment decisions and policies for both client and corporate funds, and any investment decisions involving a major shareholder, affiliated company, or a company with which any director, officer or employee is affiliated.

Although appointed president and chief executive officer only in August 1983, by October of that year Mr. Cornelissen had, according to his message in the annual report, completed a clearly defined and detailed business plan that had been approved by the board of directors. In addition, he announced that:

> Policies and objectives for all business segments were defined. Lines of communication have been shortened and simplified to ensure a closeness of senior management to products and services, and to the needs of clients. We have increased our expectations of the standards of performance of our employees and advisors.

If the above were not enough, Cornelissen also announced in the same annual report that there would be a management share purchase plan to commit senior management to shareholder interests, namely:

> The board of directors has approved a share purchase plan and a share option plan subject to approval by the shareholders at the annual meeting. The plans are designed to ensure senior management

commitment to the long-term strategic goals and objectives of the company in a manner consistent with shareholder interests.

The annual report for 1984 had Hartland Molson MacDougall give the chairman's report. The previous chairman, Eyton, resigned in October 1984. MacDougall mentioned that Royal Trust had advantages because its parent, Trilon, also owned London Life, Wellington Insurance, and Royal LePage. He did not elaborate or explain these advantages.

Cornelissen's 1984 president's message announced that five important initiatives were undertaken during the past year: (1) a commitment to quality, (2) the arrest and reverse of the past erosion in market share suffered in certain major product lines, (3) a major catch-up with necessary expenditures in computer systems development and marketing, (4) the conservative recapitalization of the company, and (5) the development of a new business planning process. The latter initiative was done by restructuring — i.e., a separation of the company's operations into personal financial services and corporate financial services — in order to be closer to the customer. Cornelissen announced that this would reduce up to five layers of management throughout the company. He also announced six new senior executives, and that an "innovative" employee compensation plan had been designed for implementation in 1985 to "ensure that deserving employees are well rewarded for superior performance against high expectations and standards we set for ourselves." No other details were given.

MacDougall noted in the 1985 annual report that there was a "new Royal Trust" that was bolder and stronger,

> ...with a board of directors who represent the highest standards of business practice and ethics, and a senior management who have established not only clear objectives but also the strategies for achieving our priorities. I am fully confident that the new Royal Trust, with its direct focus on people — our managers, employees, shareholders, and especially, our clients — is well prepared to achieve our goal of being Canada's premier provider of financial services.

Cornelissen's message for the 1985 annual report reiterated his earlier commitment to quality, market focus, and computer systems. He also noted the goal to improve linkages with other members of the Trilon group of companies. He elaborated on the pay for performance programs, which he called "unique." Specifically, he noted that there were three incentive plans — the management incentive option, the employee bonus plan, and the employee share thrift plan — and that they were an integral part of the company's performance management process. Otherwise, few specific details were given about these programs.

MacDougall announced in his 1986 annual report message that the company established a representative office in Tokyo, and, most significantly, acquired Dow Financial Services Corporation. Dow added to the company's asset management and merchant and private banking services in Switzerland, U.K., Hong Kong and Singapore. Cornelissen announced that the acquisition of Dow more than doubled the company's international operations. He also announced the four major objectives of the current five-year plan: (1) to substantially increase deposits, (2) to double mortgage lending activities, (3) to increase fee income from personal and corporate financial services to 50 percent of net income, and (4) to achieve 15 percent growth in earnings per common share while maintaining conservative capital ratios consistent with high credit ratings. These objectives were to be achieved by investing in technology to create cost-efficient deposit, lending and trust systems; obtaining new and improved branch locations, domestically and overseas; and further exploiting opportunities within the Trilon group of companies. Towards the end of his message, Cornelissen noted succinctly that the expansion would need to come from new sources: "[t]he planned 15 percent earnings growth and 15 to 20 percent return on equity means business growth will have to come, in part, from new and different sources in the years to come."

The most significant part of MacDougall's 1987 chairman's letter was not the content but the quote from a brokerage firm inserted in the margin:

> ...[S]hareholders' interests are shared by senior management whose compensation combines significant share ownership with modest fixed salaries. This arrangement reaffirms management's commitment to long-term earnings growth.

The comment came from an analyst from Walwyn, Stodgell Cochran Murray, who apparently favourably viewed the Royal Trust management incentive program for managers. It appears the chairman, MacDougall, thought this approval was important to communicate to shareholders. In other words, the chairman appeared to want to communicate the stock market's approval of Royal Trust's incentive program for managers.

Cornelissen's message stressed the successes of Royal Trust. The quotes in the margin of his president's message communicated what he apparently thought was important. The Canadian Bond Rating Service was quoted as saying:

> [Royal Trust's] primary strength has been their ability to maintain consistent growth in earnings over the past five years while maintaining a quality oriented balance sheet. Throughout this time period profitability ratios have been superior to the industry average despite their conservative leverage ratios and accounting policies.

Andreas Research Capital Inc. was quoted as saying:

> [Royal Trust] management has a sense of purpose and vision of the future and a credible plan to maximize the company's potential that are unparalleled in the financial services industry in Canada. Moreover, the company's senior management has greater rewards for superior achievement and greater penalties for failure than that of any other financial services company.

On the page following Cornelissen's report, there was a Walwyn, Stodgell Cochran Murray quote:

> In 1983, [Royal Trust] brought a new 'entrepreneurial driven' senior management who have concentrated on creating a more productive culture. The company's organizational structure was simplified making it less bureaucratic than it was before and much less than its main competitors, the banks.

MacDougall and Cornelissen announced another good year in the 1988 annual report. The latter explained these good results with the following:

> Royal Trust's sixth consecutive year of record performance again results from the hard work, enthusiasm and energy of our employees. We foster a corporate culture which lets our people's talents and initiatives flourish. The glue that binds us is our shared values. ... We shun hierarchies and bureaucracy. We encourage

and reward team players who are willing to take soundly based risks with personal accountability for results. We operate through informal networks and work groups defined by clients' needs rather than internal organization considerations.

This explanation for the successful year was similar to that given by Cornelissen in the prior year. Expansion activities were also described by Cornelissen. This included the introduction of private banking services in Montreal, Toronto, and Vancouver; and new banking, investment and trust operations in Austria, Luxembourg, the British Virgin Islands, the Isle of Man and the Barbados. Furthermore, after the year end (February 6, 1989) Royal Trust acquired Pacific First Financial Corporation of Tacoma, Washington in the United States. Cornelissen also reported on the company's performance against objectives. Apparently all objectives had been achieved in the past year.

For the second year, Cornelissen's report included quotes from market watchers. For example, Wood Gundy Inc. was quoted saying:

> [Royal Trust] is an outstanding, full-service financial services company which should continue to prosper in the de-regulated marketplace. Given the company's strategy and its management's strong personal and financial commitment to company goals, [Royal Trust]'s business fundamentals are excellent.

The Financial Post was quoted as saying:

> Like a well-oiled machine, [Royal Trust] of Toronto continues to produce steady growth in revenue and earnings with enviable consistency.

Instead of a message from the chairman in the 1989 annual report, there was a tribute to him entitled, "Royal Trust's Secret Weapon." The subtitle read, "Far from using his chairmanship to slow his pace, Hartland MacDougall now works harder than ever." The tribute ended with the following:

> That he is modest about these accomplishments is indicative of a basic humility evident in his every action. He believes honesty and integrity are the most important values in his business. This may explain, in part, his forthrightness. Untiring, enthusiastic and personable, Hartland

MacDougall is indeed Royal Trust's "secret weapon."

Cornelissen's message to the shareholders summarized the great successes that had occurred for Royal Trust since 1983.

The 1990 annual report had some differences. MacDougall and Cornelissen were now calling themselves, respectively, managing partner, chairman and managing partner, chief executive officer. MacDougall and Cornelissen started the annual report with a "partner tribute," where they admitted that "1990 was the toughest year we have faced since we joined Royal Trust" and that they were proud of "the tireless dedication and loyalty of our employee partners." They then discussed how the "partnership" led "Royal Trusters" to more effectively work together to meet client needs:

> Partnership evolved naturally from our non-bureaucratic, flat organizational structure that allows us to be immediately responsive to client needs. It empowers every partner to break down any barrier that blocks his or her ability to provide superior service. In 1990, partnership changed the way we think about each other and the way we work together.

The 1990 annual report also signalled the use of new terms for describing organizational positions; the traditional job titles of vice-president, director and manager were replaced with managing partner, partner and associate partner. In a section beside the partner tribute, these new titles were described as connoting an individual's level of accountability.

In his chairman's message, MacDougall put the bulk of the blame for poor performance on the "rapidly deteriorating economic conditions in Canada and the United Kingdom." This justification was evident in explaining the problem with the U.K. business:

> Our policy was to be conservative and risk averse. However, some of the loans we made then could not withstand the rigours of a downturn. Skyrocketing interest rates, inflation and a severely depressed real estate market resulted in problem loans for the entire U.K. banking system and we unfortunately were no exception.

In his message, Cornelissen noted that Royal Trust was "solid to the core" and that the loss of $65 million, or $1.20 per share, was the result of several factors: (1) a cyclical economy leading to an increase in mortgage defaults; (2) a combination of prolonged high rates and a steeply depressed property market in the U.K., bringing with it massive loan losses throughout the entire U.K. banking industry; (3) a severe decline in the Japanese stock market that caused investment losses in Switzerland; (4) deterioration in the value of a portfolio of U.S. equities created in 1987 to build relationships with the management of those companies.

In the 1991 annual report, MacDougall noted that 1992 would be a year of opportunity and that it was 100 years since Royal Trust was granted a charter, and 92 years since it opened its first branch. However, he said little about the past year's performance of the company.

Cornelissen said in his message to the shareholders that 1991 was one of the most difficult years for many industries as they experienced the rigours of the worst economic recession since World War II. The year, he said, was devoted to focusing on improving credit controls, reducing expenses, and building on existing strengths. More significant steps were included: restructuring European operations and the discontinuation of certain new construction loans in California. He also included Royal Trust's statement on culture and values, which emphasized entrepreneurial behaviour and adherence to the goals of the owners.

In the annual report for 1992, there was a joint message to shareholders by MacDougall and James Miller, the new president and chief executive officer (the managing partner titles were, apparently, no longer used by the chairman and president). They tersely reported a net loss of $852 million, compared with net income of $107 million for the previous year. On a common share basis, the loss was $5.93. They blamed the losses on economic conditions. They also noted:

> ...the Corporation retained S.G. Warburg to carry out an extensive review of the Corporation's operations and condition and to assist the Corporation, with the co-operation of Trilon Financial Corporation, the Corporation's largest shareholder, in assessing financial alternatives for the Corporation. It was hoped that a major financial institution would be willing to inject substantial new capital into the Corporation and a large number of financial institutions were approached on this basis.
>
> Although a direct investment could not be arranged, the Corporation successfully entered into an Agreement in Principle with Royal Bank of Canada

in mid-March, under which Royal Bank has agreed in principle to purchase most of the Corporation's Canadian and international operations. A committee of independent directors has been formed to make a recommendation to the board with respect to the fairness of the proposed transaction to security holders.

The Agreement in Principle with Royal Bank has stabilized Royal Trust's business and has allowed the Corporation to direct its efforts toward regaining some of the business lost during 1992 and early 1993. We firmly believe that the Royal Bank deal was the best deal available to the Corporation and is far better than the alternatives.

With no indication of responsibility or regret, that was the last annual report of Royal Trust.

After reviewing the annual reports, you want to assure yourself that there was a recession in 1990–1992, as stated by MacDougall and Cornelissen in their annual report messages. They had blamed the demise of Royal Trust on the recession. You examine a book from your economics course, *Self-Organizing Economy* by Paul Krugman, which says all of the major industrial countries shared the recessions of 1974–1975, 1979–1982, and 1990–1992. Statistics Canada shows the quarterly growth in gross domestic product in constant dollars for each of those recessions in the table shown in Exhibit 1.

You know that recessions are defined by quarters of negative growth. With only one quarter of negative growth, there was not really a recession during the 1974–1975 period. There were six quarters of negative growth with the 1979 to 1982 recession, and only four quarters of negative growth in the 1990–1992 recession. The data negates the statement by MacDougall and Cornelissen about the seriousness of the 1990–1992 recession.

You analyzed the Royal Trust balance sheets and income statements in Exhibit 2, and compiled the Excel spreadsheet in Exhibit 3. You noted that there were two main businesses. There was the fiduciary business when Royal Trust was looking

EXHIBIT 1: QUARTERLY GROWTH OF GDP					
Recession	**Year**	**1st**	**2nd**	**3rd**	**4th**
1974–1975	1974	1.0	0.3	0.9	0.6
	1975	–0.4	1.1	1.4	0.7
1979–1982	1979	1.1	1.3	0.5	1.2
	1980	0.4	–0.4	–0.9	1.2
	1981	2.5	0.9	–0.7	–0.5
	1982	–0.8	–1.4	–0.9	–0.9
1990–1991	1990	0.7	–0.3	–0.6	–0.9
	1991	–1.3	0.2	0.4	0.3
	1992	0.0	0.2	0.3	0.4

after the assets of others. This business showed up as fee and other income on the income statement. As the assets belonged to clients, they were not shown on Royal Trust's balance sheet. The other was the lending business, which meant money was raised through deposits and other forms of debt and equity, and then loaned or invested in securities, mortgages, loans and other investments. The revenue from this latter business was described as investment income. However, interest expenses and the provision for loan losses were subtracted from investment income to yield net investment income.

With your analysis you calculated the margin on investments and gross yield on average funds in use, and undertook other analyses. You also examined the 1983 to 1992 movement of Royal Trust common share prices, on the premise that the efficient market hypothesis predicted that share prices reflected all information about a firm. In other words, the share prices would have reflected important information about the health of a firm that was not contained in the annual reports or otherwise disclosed by the directors.

Exhibit 4 contains the share prices from 1983 to 1992. You discovered that the common prices of Royal Trust declined to virtually zero in 1993.

Your reading of the annual reports, financial statements, and stock price changes leads you to several opinions contrary to the narrative comments espoused in annual reports by the chairmen and presidents.

EXHIBIT 2: FINANCIAL STATEMENTS

Consolidated Balance Sheet
($ millions)

	1992	1991	1990	1989	1988	1987	1986	1985	1984	1983	1982
ASSETS											
Cash and short-term investments	3,131	3,715	4,958	5,567	5,310	4,279	3,453	2,146	2,070	2,107	2,235
Securities	2,905	5,364	5,470	5,875	3,920	3,616	2,530	1,862	1,621	1,016	1,684
Mortgages, loans, investments	17,790	27,320	29,394	27,475	18,838	16,244	13,068	9,217	7,278	6,344	5,594
Other assets	417	1,127	1,124	909	444	379	295	228	188	167	280
Net assets of discontinued U.S. operations	871										
Total Assets	25,114	37,526	40,946	39,826	28,512	24,518	19,346	13,453	11,157	9,634	9,793
LIABILITIES AND SHAREHOLDERS' EQUITY											
Deposits and debt	22,484	33,798	37,127	36,358	25,906	22,372	17,566	12,010	10,128	9,048	9,248
Other Liabilities, deferred taxes	234	278	280	243	235	271	224	295	226	149	129
Total Liabilities	22,718	34,076	37,407	36,601	26,141	22,643	17,790	12,305	10,354	9,197	9,377
Minority interest	9	8	7	26	42	53	58	17	21	5	6
Subordinated notes and capital debentures	1,419	1,486	1,490	921	661	196	207	—	—	—	—
Shareholders' equity	968	1,956	2,042	2,278	1,668	1,626	1,291	1,131	777	432	410
Total Liabilities and Shareholders' Equity	25,114	37,526	40,946	39,826	28,512	24,518	19,346	13,453	11,152	9,634	9,793

Consolidated Statement of Income
($ millions)

	1992	1991	1990	1989	1988	1987	1986	1985	1984	1983	1982
INCOME											
Investment Income	2,476	3,348	4,916	3,685	2,763	2,218	1,828	1,470	1,204	1,065	1,255
Interest expense	2,124	2,864	3,995	2,907	2,103	1,638	1,351	1,108	987	866	1,061
Net investment income before provisions	352	484	921	778	660	580	477	362	217	199	194
Provision for loan losses	421	155	220	23	18	26	18	12	16	18	13
Net investment income (loss) after provisions for losses	(69)	329	701	755	642	554	459	350	201	181	181
Fees and other income	351	337	349	298	248	200	154	116	263	252	211
Total Income	282	666	1,050	1,053	890	754	613	466	464	433	392
OPERATING EXPENSES											
Salaries and benefits	296	281	369	268	232	187	162	131			126
Premises, computer and equipment	160	154	—	—	—	—	—	—			34
Commissions to real estate brokers/agents	—	—	30	—	—	—	—	—			84
Restructuring costs	—	—	84	—	—	—	—	—			—
Portfolio investments	—	—	—	—	—	—	—	—			—
Other	179	167	461	334	275	233	168	129			101
Total operating expenses	635	602	944	602	507	420	330	260	366	354	345
Other additions	—	—	—	—	—	—	—	—	—	—	3
INCOME (LOSS) BEFORE THE FOLLOWING	(353)	64	106	451	383	334	283	206	98	79	50
Write-off of goodwill	(93)	21	—	—	—	—	—	—	—	—	—
Sale of stock transfer/debt trusteeship businesses	—	—	—	—	—	—	—	—	—	—	—
Income (loss) before taxes, discontinued U.S. operations	(446)	85	106	451	383	334	283	206	98	79	50
Income taxes	213	19	171	186	171	146	129	93	14	18	5
Net income (loss) before discontinued operations	(659)	66	(65)	265	212	188	154	113	84	61	45
Net income (loss) from discontinued operations	(193)	41	—	—	—	—	—	—	—	—	(1)
Non-recurring Items	—	—	—	—	—	—	—	—	1	4	—
Dividends on non-convertible preferred shares	—	—	—	—	—	—	—	35	19	10	—
Dividends on Series A and B convertible preferred shares	—	—	—	—	—	—	—	—	2	3	—
Net income (loss) applicable to preferred shareholders	(55)	71	(86)	74	56	58	51	35	21	13	10
Net income (loss) applicable to common shareholders	(907)	36	(151)	191	156	130	103	78	64	52	34
Net income (loss) after income taxes	(852)	107	(65)	265	212	188	154	113	85	65	44
Average number of shares outstanding (000,000's)	153	145	125	112	105	102	94	83	77	70	70
Earnings (loss) per common share — basic ($)	(5.93)	0.25	(1.21)	1.71	1.48	1.28	1.10	0.94	0.83	0.74	0.49

EXHIBIT 3: VARIOUS ANALYSES

	1992	1991	1990	1989	1988	1987	1986	1985	1984	1983
Margin (net investment income/investment income)	(0.028)	0.098	0.143	0.205	0.232	0.250	0.251	0.239	0.167	0.170
Gross yield on average funds in use	0.093	0.099	0.144	0.131	0.130	0.125	0.137	0.147	0.148	0.146
Interest cost (including losses)	0.095	0.089	0.124	0.104	0.100	0.094	0.103	0.112	0.123	0.121
Net yield on average funds in use	(0.003)	0.010	0.021	0.027	0.030	0.031	0.034	0.035	0.025	0.025
Rate of growth, securities, mortgages, loans, investments	(0.369)	(0.063)	0.045	0.465	0.146	0.273	0.408	0.245	0.209	0.011

EXHIBIT 4: MONTHLY STOCK PRICE ACTIVITIES ($)

	1992	1991	1990	1989	1988	1987	1986	1985	1984	1983	1982
High price	9.38	11.25	16.13	19.38	17.63	18.50	17.32	11.88	9.20	7.38	5.10
Low price	2.40	7.77	8.13	15.88	12.75	11.00	10.75	8.88	5.94	4.75	2.88
Close for Year	2.94	8.00	9.00	17.88	16.38	13.88	14.82	11.75	9.00	7.38	4.97

Note: Share pries were adjusted in splits

SBS Books

SBS is one of North America's largest book retailers. In the early 1980s it was formed by the amalgamation of two established booksellers that had 90 stores in regional malls. Subsequently SBS expanded into a wider variety of retail outlets. There are now 27 superstores, 800 mall stores, and 85 campus bookstores.

The mall stores are 4,000 to 5,000 square feet each and profitable, but they have little chance of above-average growth. The campus stores are less profitable, but with average profitability they provide advertisement for SBS's other stores. It is the superstores that Dino Giovanni, the president and chief executive officer, expects to provide SBS's growth during the next decade. He is so confident that he changed the firm's name to SBS (for Superbook Stores). And in the last two years, he has experimented with a number of concepts to make the superstores exciting places to be and thereby attractive to customers.

Dino's superstore idea calls for 40,000 square foot destination book stores. Books are sold at discounts of 10 to 40 percent, and each store may have a many as 100,000 titles. Variations to the base store that have been tested include a juvenile book section, a children's book section, a children's activity centre with supervised baby sitting, a restaurant, and an espresso bar. Although stores will vary because of the exact location and premises, the following describes the envisaged superstore:

	sq. ft.
Base store	27,000
Juvenile section increment	4,000
Children section increment	3,000
Children's activity centre	1,500
Restaurant	3,000
Espresso bar	1,500
	40,000

Real estate is purchased and/or developed to superstore specifications, and then sold to various pension funds. These properties are, in turn, rented. The belief is that SBS can earn above-average return as a book retailer, but property ownership can only yield average returns. Moreover, SBS does not want to tie up its limited financial resources in real estate.

This lack of land and buildings means that there are minimal fixed assets on the balance sheet. The only significant item is leasehold improvement, which individual store managers have no control over. Moreover, cash management, regarding cash balances, accounts receivable, accounts payable, and bank loans, is done entirely by the treasurer. As there is a lack of influence over most balance sheet items, the return on investment (ROI) measure for performance at the store level has come to be calculated as operational income (before interest expenses, corporate allocations, and income taxes) divided by average annual book inventory. Currently, Dino is requiring all aspects of the superstores to earn at least a 20 percent ROI. This demanding target necessitates a skilful blend of profit margin on sales and inventory turnover. There is concern that ROI may not always be appropriate for measuring performance.

As a corporate management accountant, you have been assigned to analyze the profitability of the base store and the variations, and make recommendations to Dino on the size and composition of the superstores and the exclusive use of ROI. You have gathered the following information, which is believed to be representative of future potentials.

Base Store

Sales	$9,450,000
Cost of goods sold	5,670,000
Gross margin	3,780,000
Wages, administration, rent, utilities	3,240,000
Operational income	$ 540,000
Sales to average book inventory	7

Juvenile Section

Revenue	$1,100,000
Cost of goods sold	605,000
Gross margin	495,000
Wages, administration, rent, utilities	445,000
Operational income	$ 50,000
Sales to average book inventory	5

Children's Section

Sales	$720,000
Cost of goods sold	432,000
Gross margin	288,000
Wages, administration, rent, utilities	280,000
Operational income	$ 8,000
Sales to average book inventory	4

Children's Activity Centre

Revenue	$ 125,000
Wages, administration, rent, utilities	240,000
Operational income	$(115,000)

The average charge is $5 per child. On average the parent(s) of each child was found by a survey to have bought $10 worth of books strictly because of the babysitting offered by the children's activity centre. The variable costs of these books are 70 percent of the sales value.

Restaurant

Sales	$525,000
Food, supplies	210,000
Wages, administration, rent, utilities	400,000
Operational income	$(85,000)

The average bill was $9 per customer. On average each of these customers was found by a survey to have bought $10 worth of books strictly because of the restaurant. The variable costs of these books are 70 percent of the sales value.

Espresso Bar

Sales	$300,000
Food, supplies	90,000
Wages, administration, rent, utilities	260,000
Operational income	$(50,000)

The average bill was $6 per customer. On average each of these customers was found by a survey to have bought $15 worth of books strictly because of the espresso bar. The variable costs of these books are 70 percent of the sales value.

Required As the corporate management accountant, perform the duties assigned by the president. Use the case approach for this assignment.

Southern Computer Machines

Four decades ago, Southern Computer Machines (SCM) started as a manufacturer of semiconductors. However, two decades ago, SCM moved into PC manufacturing as a means of reducing the impact of cyclical semiconductor sales. Now with two successful businesses, analysts at major brokerage firms say the stock market perceives SCM to be only a PC fabricator. The market's perception leads the board of directors to question whether the present divisional structure is the most appropriate for ensuring optimal returns to shareholders' investments. They are sufficiently concerned that they have hired you as a consultant to address the questions of whether the semiconductor division should be (1) kept as currently operated, (2) sold outright, (3) sold through an initial public offering (IPO) to the public, or (4) spun off by distributing the shares to existing shareholders.

You soon learn from a review of the literature and brokerage reports that since its inception, the semiconductor industry has never been able to defy business cycles that swing wildly between boom and bust. Although chip sales have increased at a steady 17 percent rate annually compounded, manufacturing capacity has grown in fits and starts, always lagging behind or exceeding demand. The present boom, which dates back two years, is no exception. For this year, analysts are projecting a 77 percent semiconductor industry-wide profit surge. Until a few weeks ago, most analysts on Bay Street and Wall Street assumed that good times would last two more years, or until chip capacity outpaces demand. Prices would then decline substantially. Nevertheless, short-term indicators were positive. Most chips were in severe shortage and prices were holding firm or trending up. Simultaneously the Philadelphia Semiconductor Stock Index jumped 68 percent in the six months that ended two weeks ago.

Then, early last week, two Wall Street chip analysts cautioned that the industry could peak within six months. Among the warning signs noted by the analysts were creeping inventory levels, scattered price declines, and shorter waits to obtain some parts. Other Wall Street and Bay Street analysts fired back with counter-arguments, but to little avail; semiconductor stocks fell 20 percent on the Philadelphia Semiconductor Stock Index in the past week. One Bay Street analyst summed up the situation, "This is a cyclical industry, and nobody wants to be the last one out."

With further investigation you see evidence that the investors may have bailed out too early. The industry has changed to where it is no longer as monolithic as it was five years ago, when the semiconductors used in PCs set the pace. The demand has become much more diversified. Now it derives most of its growth from new markets, such as Internet equipment and consumer electronics — everything from data switches and cell phones to digital cameras and DVD players. Consequently, the past extreme cycles are unlikely to be repeated.

The semiconductor industry association has provided some forecasts that indicate attractive future sales. The association says that five years ago, microprocessor and dynamic memory chips, largely used in PCs, provided 39 percent of all semiconductor revenues. In five years from now, the association expects semiconductors for PCs to represent only 25 percent of total sales. The non-PC semiconductors will be the fastest-growing sector, especially those used in communications products and optical parts used with the Internet backbone.

Although the semiconductor division can assume responsibility for a product at any stage of development, OEMs (original equipment manufacturers) benefit most when partnering with the division in the early phases of design. Early involvement with the division's technology solutions, manufacturing and operations, and global services business unit helps to ensure a smooth, rapid and cost-effective transition from product concept to volume manufacturing. Before the division begins manufacturing any product, technology "roadmaps" are established to ensure the best decisions are made. In other words, this process ensures the assembly of functional, quality products that are efficiently manufactured, tested, and serviced.

Depending on the semiconductor product being manufactured, the division's technology solutions business unit is poised to provide a wide range of services, including design of custom-integrated circuits and design co-ordination with the respective OEM. In addition, the division has broad-level design and physical layout capabilities for chip and circuit board assembly. Due to past alliances with router, cell phone, and PC manufacturers, the division now provides a complete array of chips and related products for these market areas.

The fact that the semiconductor division and the PC division are related has created some problems for the semiconductor division. Many potential PC fabricators are reluctant to buy semiconductors from the semiconductor division when they must compete for sales with its sister PC division. Other PC fabricator customers threaten to drop the division because of its association with the PC division. In addition, many of the PC division's major customers perceive there to be an ethical quandary whenever the PC division uses chips from the semiconductor division.

The business model is unclear for the semiconductor division. The division is very good at dealing with suppliers and customers. However, it is merely mediocre with the assembly of semiconductors. This confusion is reflected in its financial performance depicted in Exhibit 1.

The PC division was started as a means of selling semiconductors. With this purpose, there was a reluctance to becoming a full-fledged manufacturing and sales firm. As a result the PC division outsourced almost everything from sales to manufacturing (except for the semiconductors that can be made by the semiconductor division), to research and development. The PC division's business model had invested significantly in supplier

---

EXHIBIT 1: FINANCIAL SUMMARY — SEMICONDUCTOR DIVISION

Balance Sheet

Current Assets			Current Liabilities		
Cash, equivalent	$ 543		Accounts payable		$ 2,146
Net receivables	1,678		Accruals		452
Inventories	2,195		Other current liabilities		848
Other current assets	326				3,446
	4,742				
Long-term Assets			Long-term Liabilities and Owners' Equity		
Other investments	878		Long-term debt		5,249
Net property, plant and equipment	4,732		Deferred income		123
Intangible assets	87		Deferred taxes		223
	5,697		Other liabilities		56
			Owners' equity		1,744
					6,993
Total	$10,439		Total		$10,439

Income Statement

Net sales		$11,757
Less: Cost of goods sold		7,054
Gross income		4,703
Less: Amortization	769	
Selling and administration	3,000	
Total		3,769
Operating income		934
Other income or expenses		(200)
Pre-tax income		734
Income taxes		235
Net income		$ 499

assets, which it then linked to its customer assets using the Internet and its organizational know-how and systems. Consequently, the PC division enables customers to access sales and service on its website. Its network of linked suppliers makes it possible for the company to efficiently tailor PC products to fit the needs of individual buyers, whether for a home-based PC for the employees, or with a global company.

Thus, the division was quick to become Web-based for sales and customer service operation. It has no traditional distribution network standing between itself and its customers. Customers are served by a telephone or an online order taker who actually works for a division of a telephone company. The order is sent to a co-ordinator — actually an employee who works for another company, Supplyex — who in turn passes the order to the relevant plant from among the division's five assembly plants around the world. At the same time, Supplyex directs parts suppliers of the required parts to the selected assembly plant. Supplyex also

directs the parcel courier to the respective plant at the predetermined time to pick up and then deliver the finished computer to the customer.

The division depends on its ability to optimize all assets that make up its business model, including relationships with employees, suppliers, investors, and customers. This clarity of business model is reflected in the PC division's financial performance, depicted in Exhibit 2.

After reviewing the semiconductor division, you suggest that the division has to clarify its business model to improve performance. It does not focus on what it does best.

Required As the consultant, specify how the semiconductor division can clarify its business model and improve profits. Also, specify the advantages and disadvantages from each of the following options: (1) keep as a division, (2) sell outright, (3) sell through an initial public offering (IPO) to the public, or (4) spin off by distributing the shares to existing shareholders.

EXHIBIT 2: FINANCIAL SUMMARY — PERSONAL COMPUTER DIVISION

Balance Sheet

Current Assets			Current Liabilities		
Cash, equivalent	$2,066		Accounts payable	$1,769	
Net receivables	1,339		Accruals	168	
Inventories	196		Other current liabilities	659	
Other current assets	240			2,596	
	3,841				
Long-term Assets			Long-term Liabilities and Owners' Equity		
Other investments	1,446		Long-term debt	254	
Net property, plant and equipment	382		Deferred income	135	
Intangible assets	66		Deferred taxes	—	
	1,894		Other liabilities	96	
			Owners' equity	2,654	
				3,139	
Total	$5,735		Total	$5,735	

Income Statement

Net sales		$12,632
Less: Cost of goods sold		9,941
Gross income		2,691
Less: Amortization	78	
Selling and administration	1,180	
Total		1,258
Operating income		1,433
Other income or expenses, net		(3)
Pre-tax income		1,430
Income taxes		393
Net income		$ 1,037

Upper Canada Wood Stoves

This is your first assignment as a consultant with the prestigious McHenry Consulting firm. You want to do well. Three years ago you graduated with a business degree, and last month you earned your accounting designation. McHenry hired you last week and after getting familiarized with McHenry's business model and practices, you have been assigned to a new client, Upper Canada Wood Stoves.

Upper Canada Wood Stoves was established in 1810 as a family business. It was a booming business for its first century, but during the 20th century sales declined with the replacement of wood stoves with oil, natural gas, electricity, and central heating. Actually, the company nearly disappeared on more than one occasion. For the last two decades, the company produced only one model, called the Traditional Canadian wood stove. With this improvement in business, the owners saw an opportunity for a more contemporary model, called the Airtight Canadian. This new model is focused on customers using wood, at their cottages and country homes, as an alternative source of energy for cooking and heating.

In each of the first three years on the market, Airtight's sales met expectations. Company profits were, however, less than expected. It was unclear if the Airtight stoves were really profitable.

Sales for the latest year, shown in Exhibit 1, were for 15,000 traditional stoves at $1,000 each and 1,000 airtight stoves at $3,500 each. The company had calculated profitability in its normal method, as shown in Exhibit 2. The new airtight stoves were, accordingly, an outstanding success. On the other hand, profitability of the traditional stove had become dismal, which was difficult for the CEO to understand as it had been considered a successful stove up until the introduction of the airtight stove.

The results in Exhibit 2 were being questioned by the CEO. She recognized that profitability per stove had always been determined by gross profits

EXHIBIT 1: INCOME STATEMENTS JUNE 30 ($ 000s)

(Traditional and Airtight)

REVENUE		18,500
COST OF GOODS SOLD		
Direct materials	6,800	
Direct labour	2,400	
Factory overhead	5,800	
		15,000
GROSS PROFIT		3,500
SELLING AND ADMINISTRATION		
Selling	1,200	
Administration	1,000	
		2,200
NET INCOME BEFORE TAXES		1,300

EXHIBIT 2: PROFITABILITY ANALYSIS, PER STOVE

	Traditional Stove	Airtight Stove
Revenue	$1,000.00	$3,500.00
Cost of goods sold*	937.50	937.50
Gross margin	62.50	2,562.50

* $15,000,000/16,000

per stove, i.e., by dividing the company's gross profits by the number of stoves sold.

The CEO had considered raising the price of the traditional stove to improve profits, but had delayed that decision for two reasons. First, the traditional stove was already competitively priced in its market. Market research had indicated that price increases would be met with even larger declines in units sold. Second, she wanted to get advice on product costing and product profitability. In the past, with one product, it was obvious that product profitability was synonymous with the company's profits. However, with two products the CEO thought that a new method might be needed for product costing and for determining product profitability. Consequently, your consulting firm was engaged.

After reviewing Exhibits 1 and 2 and understanding the CEO's concerns, you realized that more cost information is needed, and you in detail asked for and received the information contained in Exhibits 3, 4, 5.

Required Use the case approach to address the CEO's requirements. Be sure to explain your analyzes and recommendations.

EXHIBIT 3: DIRECT COSTS PER STOVE

	Traditional Stove	**Airtight Stove**
Direct materials	$400	$800
Direct labour	8 hours of unskilled labour at $15 per hour	24 hours of skilled labour at $25 per hour

---

EXHIBIT 4: FACTORY OVERHEAD, BY ACTIVITY

Activities	Costs	Cost Driver
Material related	$1,500,000	These costs are associated with the administration and physical movement of parts around the factory. The number of parts in each stove, traditional and airtight, was 20 and 40, respectively.
Labour related	1,300,000	Overhead costs (such as utilities, equipment depreciation, etc.) that are incurred to support the time consuming activities of cutting, welding, sanding, assembly, and packaging.
Paint Setup	800,000	Traditional stoves were made in batches of 3,000; airtight stoves were made in batches of 200 stoves. The number of setups drove these costs.
Painting	1,400,000	Painting costs were incurred equally per stove.
Human resources	800,000	Number of people employed in production drive human resource administration and benefits.
	$5,800,000	

EXHIBIT 5: OTHER OVERHEAD

Activities	Costs	Cost Driver
Selling	$1,200,000	It was estimated that 10 percent of these costs were incurred for the traditional stoves, while 90 percent were incurred for the airtight stoves.
Administrations	$1,000,000	It was estimated that each brand — traditional and Airtight — uses 10 percent of these resources. The remaining 80 percent supports the overall company.

Wilcox Microwaves by Marcela Porporato

Wilcox has been making microwaves for almost 25 years. Currently the company's line includes 10 models, ranging from a basic model to a deluxe stainless steel model. Most of its sales are made through independent retailers, which gives the microwaves an image of high quality and associated high price. Industry sales, and those of Wilcox, have been falling in the past two years. Currently, Wilcox is selling 80,000 units per year at an average price of $120 each, with variable unit costs of $60 (of which materials are $30). As a result Wilcox is operating its plant at about 80 percent of a one-shift capacity. The last balance sheet, in thousands of dollars, is reflected in Exhibit 1.

Oh Mart, a chain of discount department stores, approached you, the general manager for sales, about the possibility of producing microwaves for them. The microwaves will be sold under the Oh Mart house brand "Big Value." They are offering a five-year contract that can be automatically extended on a year-to-year basis, unless one party gives the other at least a three-months notice to terminate the contract. The order is for 24,000 units per year with a unit price of $90 each. Oh Mart does not want title on the microwaves to pass from Wilcox to Oh Mart until the microwaves are shipped from one of its regional warehouses to a specific Oh Mart store. Additionally, Oh Mart wants the Big Value microwaves to be somewhat different in appearance from Wilcox's other micro-

waves. These requirements would increase Wilcox's purchasing, inventorying and production costs.

To decide whether or not to accept Oh Mart's offer, you gather the following additional information:

1. First year costs of producing Big Value microwaves:

Materials (include items specific to Oh Mart models)	$40
Labour	20
Overhead at 100% of labour (50% is variable; the 100% rate is based on a volume of 100,000 units per year)	20
Total unit cost	$80

2. Big Value microwaves-related added inventories (the cost of financing them is eight percent per year):
   - *Materials:* two month's supply (a total of 4,000 units);
   - *Work in process:* 1,000 units, half completed (but all materials for them issued);
   - *Finished goods:* 500 units (awaiting next carload lot shipment to an Oh Mart).

3. Impact on Wilcox's regular sales:
   Wilcox sales over the next two years will be about 84,000 units a year if it rejects the Oh Mart deal. If Wilcox accepts it, it would lose

---

EXHIBIT 1: BALANCE SHEET

Cash	$ 300	Accounts payable	$ 500
Accounts receivable	1,000	Short-term debt	2,600
Inventory	2,500	Long-term debt	1,500
Plant and		Total Liabilities	4,600
Equipment (net)	4,000	Owners equity	3,200
Total Assets	$7,800	Total	$7,800

about 6,000 units of the regular sales volume a year since their retail distribution is quite strong in Oh Mart market regions. These estimates do not include the possibility that a few of Wilcox's current dealers might drop their line if they find out Wilcox is making microwaves for Oh Mart with a lower selling price.

Required Use the case approach to analyze the short-term and long-term economic effects of the Oh Mart offer.

Yoour University

Your first job was with Barnard Bensen LLP. Although you were hired to pursue a CA, you decided after a week that your preference was for enterprise business systems technology and strategic financial management. Consequently, you obtained your CMA designation and sought all possible enterprise business systems technology assignments, especially those involving front end, customer-facing applications such as customer relationship management (CRM). Now you are a manager at Barnard Bensen in the customer solutions practice.

CRM systems and other related software allow organizations to automate and increase the efficiency of their front offices. The front office deals with an organization's acquisition and retention of, and interaction and personalized transactions with, customers, as opposed to the back office or the behind-the-scenes systems that deal with production, logistics, administration, and accounting. These back office systems are powered by enterprise resource planning systems, such as PeopleSoft and SAP. Customer-facing applications ensure that staff on the front lines have easy access to customer histories, interactions, and transactions. They also provide for customer self-service capabilities through interactive voice, data and Internet channels. Specialist CRM software links together all of these parts of the business and allows staff at all levels of the organization to see up-to-the-second customer information on a continuous basis.

A customer database or, more precisely, a data warehouse is utilized to implement CRM systems. Data warehouses contain all customer information to support real-time analyses that assist in managing the customer relationship at all touch points or points of interaction with customers — Web, telephone, e-mail, and face-to-face, plus point-of-sale, billing, or other operational systems — both inbound and outbound. CRM makes sure that customers are treated the same, regardless of how they are interacting with the organization. For example, if a customer contacts a call centre with a service complaint, the call-centre representative can see that the customer has a large order pending and expedite the order to keep the customer satisfied. In this way, CRM is called database marketing.

Specifically, the CRM data warehouse contains details on customers, names, addresses, when and what they have purchased, when and why they have contacted the organization, how they have responded to advertisements and promotions, etc. A data warehouse should have all information on all customers, and ideally it should maintain information on prospective customers as well as past customers.

CRMs are important for three reasons. First, customers are an organization's most valuable asset. Each customer on the list is expensive and time-consuming to acquire. Past customers are the most likely to be future customers. Second, most organizations do a poor job of dealing with customers. This is usually because the organization is unable to co-ordinate all of its customer touch points. Third, the Internet and information technology allow for a much greater proportion of customer interactions to be captured, co-ordinated, and delivered digitally.

Amazon.com provides an example of an organization using a CRM system. Amazon users browse the website, then order books and CDs using formatted Web pages by filling in order, personal and credit card details. Amazon's system captures all of this data, using it to push recommendations based on customers' buying histories. Customer files are used to automatically send e-mails on the status of orders, and to mass-market new services like auctions. Furthermore, if customers are browsing travel books on, for example, Jamaica, Amazon's system can flash up a recommendation for a Bob Marley CD, with one-click ordering. Moreover, Amazon has a complete record of a customer's e-mails and its own responses. Amazon also collects data on which promotions work and which do not.

CRM systems allow organizations to collect and analyze customer data and, in some cases, initiate real-time responses. Older CRM software packages or operational applications are limited to gathering data from customer interactions such as service calls, sales transactions, and website activity. The newer CRM software packages include analytical applications that evaluate customer data for patterns that assist with the development of marketing campaigns and targeted sales pitches. CRM systems are able to integrate all touch points, whether telephone, Internet, or personally initiated. Information for the latter is the most difficult to capture, as it often is manually inputted.

Banks are using CRM systems to put personalization back into the banking relationship. Twenty-five years ago banking was personal, face-to-face, and largely conducted in the branch. Then, through the introduction of cost-reducing automatic teller machine (ATM) technology, customer closeness was lost. Banks were able to further reduce costs by automating more transactions, but at the cost of being detached from customers. Banks use CRM technology to efficiently and effectively understand customer requirements and to respond to problems. However, banks need to be careful that the CRMs are not used primarily for cross selling other bank services.

You are the manager assigned to write the proposal for implementing a CRM (customer relationship management) system at Yoour University, the major university in the capital city where you live. You learn from the partner in charge of the information technology practice that the request for proposals (RFP) has come from Yoour University's president, who sees a need to change the way students and the university interact with administrative matters. In the RFP, there are three reasons underlying the president's desire for a CRM system. First, a CRM would reduce costs from the multitude of overlapping and expensive systems that provide an incomplete service to students. Data from organizations such as Dell citing costs per customer service interaction as $10 with personal contact, $7.50 with call centres, $2.45 with voice response systems, and $0.18 with Internet have influenced the president in her desire for a CRM system. Second, a CRM system would provide students with improved services by having a co-ordinated focus to their inquiries and transactions with the university. Third, improvements in the student experience would instill positive feelings, thereby leading them to be better donors after they graduate and become alumni members. In effect, the president wants a description of what will be subject to a CRM system. With that description,

the president can contact CRM vendors for quotations for an installed CRM system.

At a meeting arranged by the president to provide information to consulting organizations interested in submitting proposals, you learn that Yoour University has 35,000 undergraduate students and 10,000 graduate students. Back office activities are handled by an enterprise resource planning system by PeopleSoft. For the front office activities dealing with students and the focus of CRM, Yoour University has the following computerized or manual systems.

1. **Admissions.** The Admissions unit is responsible for obtaining enrolments. This is done by first recording all applicants and then accepting those who qualify, according to established criteria. This responsibility also involves communications with applicants by mail, telephone, and e-mail. It also assigns accepted students with unique identifying numbers. Manual forms are used with the admissions process.

2. **Registrar.** This unit keeps track of student academic progress with what is called the student information system. It records all grades, grade changes, reactivations, faculty transfers, course adds, course drops, etc. It interacts with students using the voice response system, the Web page, e-mail, surface mail, and telephone. The registrar unit also does a program audit once students have declared they expect to graduate, which is either at the spring or fall convocation.

   One shortcoming was noted: the student information system does not do prerequisite checks to ensure that students have the proper background for the courses they are taking. Also, a new website was launched to bring under one umbrella all existing interactive services for students. These services include not only the capacity to change an address or SIN, but also to view grades and student accounts.

   Presently, the admissions unit and the registrar's unit are located in separate buildings across campus from each other. There are plans to place both under the same roof to improve services to students.

3. **Transcripts.** Current and past students contact the registrar's unit for certified copies of their transcripts. Name and address information is not used to update student or alumni records.

4. **Financial assistance.** This unit has primary responsibility for all aspects of a student's

financial relationship with the university, including administration of provincial assistance, allocation of bursaries and scholarships, and the collection of fees. There are a number of systems involved. Recently, this unit developed a new student account statement and made it available on the Web. It also implemented Internet and telephone banking to make it easier for students to make their payments to the university without having to wait in a lineup.

5. **Residence.** Each student in residence is recorded in the residence system. The data collected include name, home address, next of kin in case of emergency, and room/apartment assignment. Also, there is a system that looks after recording the payment of various residence fees.

6. **Faculty.** Each faculty, such as Arts, Education, and Business, answers questions posed by students regarding their programs or courses, required electives, location of classes, dates for final examinations, etc. Generally this is done by a specialized unit, commonly called the office of student assistance and services. Students also contact the dean, associate dean or an administrative person on these matters. Some faculties have, on their own, established Web pages to proactively address student questions and concerns.

7. **Departments.** Each department has administrative personnel who answer questions posed by students regarding their program or courses required, electives, location of classes, dates for final examinations, submission of assignments, etc. To be proactive, some departments have established Web pages to address student questions and concerns.

8. **Alumni.** Once students graduate, they automatically become members of the Yoour University alumni. Although the names of all graduates are correctly recorded along with the degree or degrees, the addresses have not been accurately maintained. A few years ago, an organization was allowed to contact or, more often, attempt to contact all possible alumni in order to compile an alumni directory. The company was allowed to sell the directory. Yoour University benefited from up-to-date addresses for many alumni members. However, at the termination of the project, addresses were listed for only about half of the graduates, and many of those addresses were incorrect. Other than this arrangement, Yoour University has not, before or after, attempted to systematically keep track of its alumni. It is estimated that only 35 percent of the addresses are correct.

9. **Advancement.** Fundraising is done or at least co-ordinated by the Advancement unit. Careful records are maintained of all donors. This list is used for regular fundraising activities, following the argument that the best donors are those who have donated in the past.

10. **Library.** A separate record of all persons with library cards is maintained. This list is automatically updated with changes in the status of students, faculty, or staff. Alumni members are allowed to obtain library privileges at a nominal annual charge.

Required In order to prepare a proposal for designing an effective CRM system or systems, first identify the existing systems and document what they do; then design for Yoour University a CRM system or systems to address what should be done.